I0015454

iOS 9 Game Development Essentials

Design, build, and publish an iOS game from scratch using the stunning features of iOS 9

Chuck Gaffney

BIRMINGHAM - MUMBAI

iOS 9 Game Development Essentials

First published: October 2015

Production reference: 1261015

Published by Packt Publishing Ltd.
Livery Place
35 Livery Street
Birmingham B3 2PB, UK.

ISBN 978-1-78439-143-0

www.packtpub.com

Cover image by Chuck Gaffney

Credits

Author
Chuck Gaffney

Reviewers
Mohit Athwani
Rahul Borawar
Chady Kassouf
Joni Mikkola

Commissioning Editor
Julian Ursell

Acquisition Editors
Vinay Argekar
Sonali Vernekar

Content Development Editor
Parita Khedekar

Technical Editor
Edwin Moses

Copy Editor
Dipti Mankame

Project Coordinator
Judie Jose

Proofreader
Safis Editing

Indexer
Hemangini Bari

Graphics
Abhinash Sahu

Production Coordinator
Nitesh Thakur

Cover Work
Nitesh Thakur

About the Author

Chuck Gaffney is a programmer, voice actor, and game developer. He owns a company, Chuck's Anime Shrine, and has worked for some studios in New York. Some of Chuck's recent projects include VR and Unity projects for major studios and business firms, in addition to iOS and Swift programming.

I would like to thank my family for giving me my first video game system in 1985 at the young age of two. The wonder and mystery of controlling what's on the screen has stuck with me ever since. Most importantly, I would like to thank my fiancée, Danielle, for keeping me on my toes with this book and understanding the time it took to craft it. Thank you for being there through the ups and downs that come from pursuing steady and worthwhile work in the field of software development; particularly during this summer, when things finally changed after years of doing nothing but seemingly staring at closed doors and calling out to deaf ears.

About the Reviewers

Mohit Athwani is a self-taught iOS developer and has been developing apps since the early days of iOS 3. He has worked with several clients all around the world, and has carried out intense research in the field of facial detection and recognition on iOS. His app, iRajanee, became the number one app on the Indian app store, and has fetched him tremendous success.

Mohit started his company Geeks (`http://www.geeksincorporated.net`) with a friend in 2010, and has since also involved himself in conducting training sessions on iOS for students and corporates. His website, `http://indianios.guru/`, hosts a lot of introductory videos and tutorials on developing for iOS with Swift.

I would like to thank my parents for gifting me my first MacBook and iPhone that allowed me to become an iOS developer. I would like to thank my friends and everybody who have encouraged me to come up with new ideas and concepts, and Packt publishing for giving me the opportunity to review this book.

Rahul Borawar is a computer science graduate from Jodhpur Institute of Engineering and Technology in Rajasthan, India. He is a passionate software craftsman, and loves designing software for mobiles. From the start, he has been a mobile application developer creating applications for iOS and Android platforms. He has been working on mobile development since 2011 and has published many apps on the app store, such as *Catch the Aliens* (a 2D level-based game) and *Draw Your Stories* (a kids' app for creating fables with drawing stuffs). He is currently working as a software development engineer in the mobile team for a real estate product-based company (CommonFloor). He has reviewed one more book for Packt Publications, named *iOS Game Programming Cookbook*, which can be viewed at `https://www.packtpub.com/game-development/ios-game-programming-cookbook`.

You can follow him on Twitter (`https://twitter.com/RahulBorawar`) and on GitHub (`https://github.com/Rahul2389`). You can also check his website, `http://rahulborawar.branded.me`.

First of all, I would like to thank Packt Publishing for giving me the opportunity to review this technology-rich cookbook and enlighten my iOS application development skills. Secondly, thanks to my family for supporting me in my career as a technical guy.

Chady Kassouf is an independent iOS and web development expert. He started programming 23 years ago and hasn't stopped since.

Seven years ago, he decided to leave his job as a team leader in one of the leading digital agencies and start his own business.

His interests, besides computers, include arts, music, and fitness. He can be found online at `http://chady.net/`.

Joni Mikkola is currently working on his next mobile game in northern Finland. He keeps his game developing stamina up by training regularly at the gym and eating healthily. Among developing games, he often reads books, plays the piano, or bakes buns, to keep his ideas flowing and his mind focused. He constantly keeps challenging the status quo, which, in turn, helps in learning new ways to create things.

He has developed games professionally for over 4 years mostly for mobile platforms. He targets casual games and focuses on creating simplistic designs. With one game released, he is currently working on his next game, which will be released in late 2015 for Android and iOS platforms.

www.PacktPub.com

Support files, eBooks, discount offers, and more

For support files and downloads related to your book, please visit `www.PacktPub.com`.

Did you know that Packt offers eBook versions of every book published, with PDF and ePub files available? You can upgrade to the eBook version at `www.PacktPub.com` and as a print book customer, you are entitled to a discount on the eBook copy. Get in touch with us at `service@packtpub.com` for more details.

At `www.PacktPub.com`, you can also read a collection of free technical articles, sign up for a range of free newsletters and receive exclusive discounts and offers on Packt books and eBooks.

https://www2.packtpub.com/books/subscription/packtlib

Do you need instant solutions to your IT questions? PacktLib is Packt's online digital book library. Here, you can search, access, and read Packt's entire library of books.

Why subscribe?

- Fully searchable across every book published by Packt
- Copy and paste, print, and bookmark content
- On demand and accessible via a web browser

Free access for Packt account holders

If you have an account with Packt at `www.PacktPub.com`, you can use this to access PacktLib today and view 9 entirely free books. Simply use your login credentials for immediate access.

Table of Contents

Preface

Since the introduction of iOS 8 in 2014, game development for the iOS platform has gone through some major changes. The first of those changes was the introduction of the Swift programming language, a functional programming language made by Apple to be simple to code and modern in its capabilities, all while being fast enough to handle modern app and game development. iOS 8 also introduced the 3D game development framework, SceneKit. SceneKit allowed developers to quickly design 3D games and work with 3D assets in a similar fashion to iOS 7's SpriteKit. A year later, in the summer of 2015, iOS 9 was introduced, along with a new set of tools for both seasoned and brand new iOS game developers. The new framework, GameplayKit, lets developers handle the game rules, AI, game entities, and game states separately from the inheritance logic. In addition to GameplayKit, Apple showed off the Fox game example that displays how Xcode can now do much of the same visual editing functionalities seen in multiplatform game engines, such as Unity and Unreal Engine.

We will first become familiar with the Swift programming language and how it can be used in the scope of game development. The goal is to understand iOS game development from the ground up, learning the tougher code-centric methodology of making a game. In addition to taking a look at Apple's own example projects for the various iOS game frameworks, we will see some code examples from two games, the first game being a published Swift-developed 2D scrolling game named PikiPop and the other being a tile-based Minesweeper clone named SwiftSweeper. As we progress through the book, we will still keep code as the core of our method for game development, but will look into the visual tools introduced in iOS 9 that, in addition to GameplayKit and the component-based structuring, can allow us to create a game that is only limited by our imagination. We then dive into topic of the low-level APIs, such as OpenGL ES and Metal, for developers who wish to get down directly to the GPU.

In the end, we hope that you understand how iOS continues to be a power game development platform, whether you are a developer who comes from the traditional code-centric school of computer science, or you are a part of the growing visual-based/drag-and-drop design paradigm. Our goal is that when you are finished with this book, you will have a number of vastly different and detailed game ideas, which you then can immediately begin building with Swift and the iOS 9 platforms.

What this book covers

Chapter 1, *The Swift Programming Language*, provides an introduction and guidance to the Swift programming language.

Chapter 2, *Structuring and Planning a Game Using Storyboards and Segues*, helps readers know the basic flow of an iOS app by making use of storyboards and segues in order to either plan or preplan iOS games.

Chapter 3, *SpriteKit and 2D Game Design*, introduces and explains the use of the iOS 2D game development framework, SpriteKit.

Chapter 4, *SceneKit and 3D Game Design*, helps readers look into the iOS 3D development framework, SceneKit, and visual tools introduced in iOS that can be used for both SceneKit and SpriteKit.

Chapter 5, *Gameplaykit*, introduces the GameplayKit framework, a universal game logic and AI framework introduced in iOS 9.

Chapter 6, *Exhibit the Metal in your Game*, discusses about advanced topics, such as the GPU graphics pipeline and an introduction to Apple's low-level API, Metal, for getting the best performance out of your game.

Chapter 7, *Publishing Our iOS Game*, .explains the steps needed to beta test and publish iOS games by making use of the testing and quality assurance service, TestFlight.

Chapter 8, *The Future of iOS Game Development*, discusses how programming, iOS, and game development as a whole might change or improve in the near future, and how it relates to the most recent iOS platforms and frameworks.

What you need for this book

Here's what you need for this book:

- Xcode 7 or later
- Mac OS X Yosemite or later

Who this book is for

This book is intended for game developers who wish to develop 2D and 3D games for iPhone and iPad. If you are a developer from another platform or a game engine such as Android or Unity, a current iOS developer wishing to learn more about Swift and the latest features of iOS 9, or even if you are new to game development, then this book is for you. Some prior programming knowledge is recommended, but not required.

Conventions

In this book, you will find a number of text styles that distinguish between different kinds of information. Here are some examples of these styles and an explanation of their meaning.

Code words in text, filenames, file extensions, pathnames, and user input, are shown as follows: "As we can see, the `AppDelegate.swift` and the `ViewController.swift` files were automatically created for us and right below that, we'd find the `Main.Storyboard` file."

A block of code is set as follows:

```
let score = player.score
var scoreCountNum = 0

do {
    HUD.scoreText = String(scoreCountNum)
    scoreCountNum = scoreCountNum * 2
} while scoreCountNum < score
```

When we wish to draw your attention to a particular part of a code block, the relevant lines or items are set in bold:

```
// Collision bit masks
typedef NS_OPTIONS(NSUInteger, AAPLBitmask) {
    AAPLBitmaskCollision        = 1UL << 2,
    AAPLBitmaskCollectable      = 1UL << 3,
    AAPLBitmaskEnemy            = 1UL << 4,
    AAPLBitmaskSuperCollectable = 1UL << 5,
    AAPLBitmaskWater            = 1UL << 6
};
```

New terms and important words are shown in bold. Words that you see on the screen, for example, in menus or dialog boxes, appear in the text like this: " Alternately, imagine that the player lost all of their lives and got a **Game Over** message."

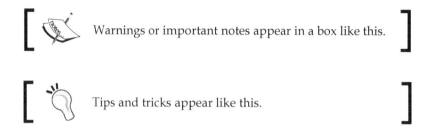

Warnings or important notes appear in a box like this.

Tips and tricks appear like this.

Reader feedback

Feedback from our readers is always welcome. Let us know what you think about this book—what you liked or disliked. Reader feedback is important for us as it helps us develop titles that you will really get the most out of.

To send us general feedback, simply e-mail feedback@packtpub.com, and mention the book's title in the subject of your message.

If there is a topic that you have expertise in and you are interested in either writing or contributing to a book, see our author guide at www.packtpub.com/authors.

Customer support

Now that you are the proud owner of a Packt book, we have a number of things to help you to get the most from your purchase.

Downloading the example code

You can download the example code files from your account at http://www.packtpub.com for all the Packt Publishing books you have purchased. If you purchased this book elsewhere, you can visit http://www.packtpub.com/support and register to have the files e-mailed directly to you.

Downloading the color images of this book

We also provide you with a PDF file that has color images of the screenshots/diagrams used in this book. The color images will help you better understand the changes in the output. You can download this file from `http://www.packtpub.com/sites/default/files/downloads/iOS9_GameDevelopmentEssentials_ColorImages.pdf`.

Errata

Although we have taken every care to ensure the accuracy of our content, mistakes do happen. If you find a mistake in one of our books—maybe a mistake in the text or the code—we would be grateful if you could report this to us. By doing so, you can save other readers from frustration and help us improve subsequent versions of this book. If you find any errata, please report them by visiting `http://www.packtpub.com/submit-errata`, selecting your book, clicking on the **Errata Submission Form** link, and entering the details of your errata. Once your errata are verified, your submission will be accepted and the errata will be uploaded to our website or added to any list of existing errata under the Errata section of that title.

To view the previously submitted errata, go to `https://www.packtpub.com/books/content/support` and enter the name of the book in the search field. The required information will appear under the **Errata** section.

Piracy

Piracy of copyrighted material on the Internet is an ongoing problem across all media. At Packt, we take the protection of our copyright and licenses very seriously. If you come across any illegal copies of our works in any form on the Internet, please provide us with the location address or website name immediately so that we can pursue a remedy.

Please contact us at `copyright@packtpub.com` with a link to the suspected pirated material.

We appreciate your help in protecting our authors and our ability to bring you valuable content.

Questions

If you have a problem with any aspect of this book, you can contact us at `questions@packtpub.com`, and we will do our best to address the problem.

1
The Swift Programming Language

At the core of game development is your game's code. It is the brain of your project and outside of the art, sound, and various asset developments. It is where you will spend most of your time creating and testing your game. Up until Apple's **Worldwide Developers Conference WWDC14** in June of 2014, the code of choice for iOS game and app development was **Objective-C**. At *WWDC14*, a new and faster programming language, Swift, was announced and is now the recommended language for all current and future iOS games and general app creation.

As of the time of writing, you can still use Objective-C to design your games, but programmers, both, new and seasoned, will see why writing in Swift is not only easier for expressing your game's logic, but even more preformat. Keeping your game running at that critical 60 fps is dependent on fast code and logic. Engineers at Apple developed the Swift programming language from the ground up with performance and readability in mind, so this language can execute certain code iterations faster than Objective-C while also keeping code ambiguity to a minimum. Swift also uses many of the methodologies and syntaxes found in more modern languages, such as Scala, JavaScript, Ruby, and Python.

So, let's dive into the Swift language.

 It is recommended that some basic knowledge of object-oriented programming (OOP) be known previously, but we will try to keep the build-up and explanation of code simple and easy to follow as we move on to the more advanced topics related to game development.

Hello World!

It's somewhat traditional when learning programming languages to begin with a **Hello World** example. A Hello World program is simply using your code to display or log the text Hello World. It's always been the general starting point because sometimes just getting your code environment set up and having your code executing correctly is half the battle. At least, this was more the case in older programming languages.

Swift makes this easier than ever, and without going into the structure of a Swift file (which we shall do later on and is also much easier than Objective-C and past languages), here's how you create a Hello World program:

```
print("Hello, World!")
```

That's it! That is all you need to have the text Hello World appear in Xcode's debug area output.

No more semicolons

Those of us who have been programming for some time might note that the usually all-important semicolon (;) is missing. This isn't a mistake; in Swift, we don't have to use a semicolon to mark the end of an expression. We can if we'd like, and some of us might still do it as a force of habit, but Swift has omitted that common concern.

The use of the semicolon to mark the end of an expression stems from the earliest days of programming when code was written in simple word processors and needed a special character to represent when the code's expression ends and the next begins.

Variables, constants, and primitive data types

While programming any application, either if new to programming or trying to learn a different language, first we should get an understanding of how a language handles variables, constants, and various data types, such as Booleans, integers, floats, strings, and arrays. You can think of the data in your program as boxes or containers of information. Those containers can be of different flavors or types. Throughout the life of your game, the data can change (variables, objects, and so on) or they can stay the same.

For example, the number of lives a player has would be stored as a variable, as that is expected to change during the course of the game. That variable would then be of the primitive data type integer, which is basically whole numbers. Data that stores, say, the name of a certain weapon or power-up in your game, would be stored in what's known as a constant, as the name of that item is never going to change. In a game where the player can have interchangeable weapons or power-ups, the best way to represent the currently equipped item would be to use a variable. A variable is a piece of data that is bound to change. That weapon or power-up will also most likely have a bit more information to it than just a name or number; the primitive types we mentioned prior. The currently equipped item would be made up of properties, such as its name, power, effects, index number, and the sprite or 3D model that visually represents it. Thus, the currently equipped item wouldn't just be a variable of a primitive data type, but be what is known as a type of object. Objects in programming can hold a number of properties and functionalities that can be thought of as a *black box* of both function and information. The currently equipped item in our case would be a sort of *placeholder* that can hold an item of that type and interchange it when needed, fulfilling its purpose as a replaceable item.

> Swift is what's known as a *type-safe language*, so we should keep track of the exact type of data and even it's future usage (that is, if the data is or will be NULL), as it's very important when working with Swift compared with other languages. Apple made Swift behave this way to help keep runtime errors and bugs in your applications to a minimum, so we can find them much earlier in the development process.

Variables

Let's look at how variables are declared in Swift.

```
var lives = 3      //variable of representing the player's lives
lives = 1          //changes that variable to a value of 1
```

Those of us who have been developing in JavaScript will feel right at home here. Like JavaScript, we use the keyword `var` to represent a variable, and we named the variable `lives`.

The compiler implicitly knows that the type of this variable is a whole number, the primitive data type `Int`.

The type can be explicitly declared as such:

```
var lives: Int = 3    //variable of type Int
```

We can also represent lives as the floating point data types double or float, as follows:

```
// lives are represented here as 3.0 instead of 3
var lives: Double = 3          //of type Double
var lives: Float = 3           //of type Float
```

Using a colon after the variable's name declaration allows us to explicitly typecast the variable.

Constants

During your game, there will be points of data that don't change throughout the life of the game or the game's current level/scene. These can be various data, such as gravity, a text label in the **Heads-Up Display (HUD)**, the center point of character's 2D animation, an event declaration, or the time before your game checks for new touches/swipes.

Declaring constants is almost the same as declaring variables.

Using a colon after the variable's name declaration allows us to explicitly typecast the variable.

```
let gravityImplicit  = -9.8          //implicit declaration
let gravityExplicit: Float  =  -9.8 //explicit declaration
```

As we can see, we use the keyword let to declare constants.

Here's another example using a string that could represent a message displayed on the screen at the start or end of a stage:

```
let stageMessage  = "Start!"
stageMessage       = "You Lose!"    //error
```

Since the string stageMessage is a constant, we cannot change it once it has been declared. Something like this would be better as a variable using var instead of let.

 "Why don't we declare everything as a variable?"

This is a question sometimes asked by new developers and is understandable why it's asked, especially since game apps tend to have a large number of variables and more interchangeable states than an average application. When the compiler is building its internal list of your game's objects and data, more goes on behind the scenes with variables than with constants.

Without getting too much into topics, such as the program's stack and other details, in short, having objects, events, and data declared as constants with the `let` keyword is more efficient than `var`. In a small app on the newest devices today, though not recommended, we could possibly get away with this without seeing a great deal of loss in app performance. When it comes to video games, however, performance is critical. Buying back as much performance as possible can allow a better player experience. Apple recommends that when in doubt, always use `let` at the time of declaration and have the complier say when to change to `var`.

More about constants…

As of Swift version 1.2, constants can have a conditionally controlled initial value.

Prior to this update, we had to initialize a constant with a single starting value or be forced to make the property a variable. In Xcode 6.3 and newer, we can perform the following logic:

```
let x : SomeThing

if condition
{
   x = foo()
}
else
{
   x = bar()
}
use(x)
```

An example of this in a game could be as follows:

```
let stageBoss : Boss

if (stageDifficulty == gameDifficulty.hard)
{
   stageBoss = Boss.toughBoss()
}
else
{
   stageBoss = Boss.normalBoss()
}
loadBoss(stageBoss)
```

With this functionality, a constant's initialization can have a layer of variance while still keeping it unchangeable, or immutable through its use. Here, the constant `stageBoss` can be one of two types based on the game's difficulty: `Boss.toughBoss()` or `Boss.normalBoss()`. The boss won't change for the course of this stage, so it makes sense to keep it as a constant. More on **if and else statements** is covered later in the chapter.

Arrays, matrices, sets, and dictionaries

Variables and constants can represent a collection of various properties and objects. The most common collection types are arrays, matrices, sets, and dictionaries. An array is an ordered list of distinct objects; a matrix is, in short, an array of arrays; a set is an unordered list of distinct objects; and a dictionary is an unordered list that utilizes a *key : value* association with the data.

Arrays

Here's an example of an array in Swift:

```
let stageNames : [String] = ["Downtown Tokyo","Heaven
Valley","Nether"]
```

The object `stageNames` is a collection of strings representing the names of a game's stages. Arrays are ordered by subscripts from 0 to array length -1. So, `stageNames[0]` would be `Downtown Tokyo`; `stageNames[2]` would be `Nether`; and `stageNames[4]` would give an error since that's beyond the limits of the array and doesn't exist. We use [] brackets around the class type of `stageNames`, `[String]`, to tell the compiler that we are dealing with an array of strings. Brackets are also used around the individual members of this array.

2D arrays / matrices

A common collection type used in physics calculations, graphics, and game design, particularly grid-based puzzle games, is two-dimensional arrays / matrices. 2D arrays are simply arrays that have arrays as their members. These arrays can be expressed in a rectangular fashion in rows and columns.

For example, the 4x4 (4 rows, 4 columns) tile board in the 15-puzzle game can be represented as follows:

```
var tileBoard = [[1,2,3,4],
                 [5,6,7,8],
                 [9,10,11,12],
                 [13,14,15,""]]
```

In the 15 puzzle game, your goal is to shift the tiles using the one empty spot (represented with the blank string `""`), to all end up in the 1-15 order as we saw. The game would start with the numbers arranged in a random and solvable order, and the player would then have to swap the numbers and the blank space.

> To better perform various actions on and/or store information about each tile in the 15 game (and other games), it'd be better to create a tile object as opposed to using raw values seen here. For the sake of understanding what a matrix or 2D array is, simply make a note of how the array is surrounded by doubly encapsulated brackets `[[]]`. We will later use one of our example games, `SwiftSweeper`, to better understand how puzzle games use 2D arrays of objects to create a full game.

Here are ways to declare blank 2D arrays with strict types:

```
var twoDTileArray : [[Tiles]] = []      //blank 2D array
of type,Tiles
var anotherArray = Array<Array<Tile>>()  //same array,
using Generics
```

The variable `twoDTileArray` uses the double brackets `[[Tiles]]` to declare it as a blank 2D array/matrix for the made-up type, tiles. The variable `anotherArray` is a rather oddly declared array that uses angle bracket characters `<>` for enclosures. It utilizes what's known as **Generics**. Generics is a rather advanced topic that we will touch more on later. They allow very flexible functionality among a wide array of data types and classes. For the moment, we can think of them as a catch-all way of working with objects.

To fill in the data for either version of this array, we would then use for-loops. More on loops and iterations will be explained later in the chapter.

Sets

This is how we would make a set of various game items in Swift:

```
var keyItems = Set([Dungeon_Prize, Holy_Armor, Boss_Key,"A"])
```

This set `keyItems` has various objects and a character `A`. Unlike an array, a set is not ordered and contains unique items. So, unlike `stageNames`, attempting to get `keyItems[1]` would return an error and `items[1]` might not necessarily be the `Holy_Armor` object, as the placement of objects is internally random in a set. The advantage sets have over arrays is that sets are great at checking for duplicated objects and specific content searching in the collection overall. Sets make use of hashing to pinpoint the item in the collections, so checking for items in a set's content can be much faster than in an array. In game development, a game's key items, which the player may only get once and should never have duplicates of, could work great as a set. Using the function `keyItems.contains(Boss_Key)` returns the Boolean value of `true` in this case.

Sets were added in Swift 1.2 and Xcode 6.3. Their class is represented by the generic type `Set<T>`, where `T` is the class type of the collection. In other words, the set, `Set([45, 66, 1233, 234]).` would be of the type `Set<Int>`, and our example here would be a `Set<NSObject>` instance due to it having a collection of various data types.

We will discuss more on Generics and class hierarchy later in this chapter.

Dictionaries

A dictionary can be represented this way in Swift:

```
var playerInventory: [Int : String]  =  [1 : "Buster Sword",
43 : "Potion", 22: "StrengthBooster"]
```

Dictionaries use a `key : value` association, so `playerInventory[22]` returns the value `StrengthBooster` based on the key `22`. Both the key and value could be initialized to almost any class type*. In addition to the inventory example given, we can have the following code:

```
var stageReward: [Int : GameItem] = [:] //blank initialization
//use of the Dictionary at the end of a current stage
stageReward = [currentStage.score : currentStage.rewardItem]
```

*The values of a dictionary, though rather flexible in Swift, do have limitations. The key must conform to what's known as the hashable protocol. Basic data types, such as `Int` and `String`, already have this functionality. So, if you are to make your own classes / data structures that are to be used in dictionaries, say mapping a player actions with player input, this protocol must be utilized first. We will discuss more about protocols later in this chapter.

Dictionaries are like sets in that they are unordered but with the additional layer of having a key and a value associated with their content instead of just the hash key. Like sets, dictionaries are great for quick insertion and retrieval of specific data. In iOS apps and in web applications, dictionaries are used to parse and select items from JavaScript Object Notation (JSON) data.

In the realm of game development, dictionaries using JSON or via Apple's internal data class, `NSUserDefaults`, can be used to save and load game data, set up game configurations, or access specific members of a game's API.

For example, here's one way to save a player's high score in an iOS game using Swift:

```
let newBestScore : Void =
NSUserDefaults.standardUserDefaults().setInteger(bestScore,
forKey: "bestScore")
```

This code comes directly from a published Swift-developed game named PikiPop, which we will use from time to time to show code used in actual game applications.

Again, note that dictionaries are unordered, but Swift has ways to iterate or search through an entire dictionary. We will go more in depth in the next section and later on when we move on to loops and control flow.

Mutable/immutable collections

One rather important discussion that we've left out is how to subtract, edit, or add to arrays, sets, and dictionaries. However, before we do this, you should understand the concept of mutable and immutable data/collections.

A mutable collection is simple data that can be changed, added to, or subtracted from, whereas an immutable collection cannot be changed, added to, or subtracted from.

To work with mutable and immutable collections efficiently in Objective-C, we had to explicitly state the mutability of the collection beforehand. For example, an array of the type `NSArray` in Objective-C is always immutable. There are methods we can call on `NSArray` that would edit the collection, but behind the scenes, this would be creating brand new `NSArray` objects, thus would be rather inefficient to do this often in the life of our game. Objective-C has solved this issue with the class type, `NSMutableArray`.

Thanks to the flexibility of Swift's type inference, we already know how to make a collection mutable or immutable! The concept of constants and variables has us covered when it comes to data mutability in Swift. Using the keyword `let` when creating a collection will make that collection immutable, while using `var` will initialize it as a mutable collection.

```
//mutable Array
var unlockedLevels : [Int] =  [1, 2, 5, 8]

//immutable Dictionary
let playersForThisRound : [PlayerNumber:PlayerUserName] =
[453:"userName3344xx5", 233:"princeTrunks", 6567:
"noScopeMan98", 211: "egoDino"]
```

The array of integers, `unlockedLevels`, can be edited simply because it's a variable. The immutable dictionary `playersForThisRound` can't be changed since it's already been declared as a constant. There is no additional layer of ambiguity concerning additional class types.

Editing/accessing collection data

As long as a collection type is a variable, using the `var` keyword, we can do various edits to the data. Let's go back to our `unlockedLevels` array. Many games have the functionality of unlocking levels as the player progresses. Let's say that the player has reached the high score needed to unlock the previously locked level 3 (as 3 isn't a member of the array). We can add 3 to the array using the `append` function:

```
unlockedLevels.append(3)
```

Another neat attribute of Swift is that we can add data to an array using the `+=` assignment operator:

```
unlockedLevels += [3]
```

Doing it this way however will simply add 3 to the end of the array. So, our previous array `[1, 2, 5, 8]` is now `[1, 2, 5, 8, 3]`. This probably isn't a desirable order, so to insert the number 3 in the third spot, `unlockedLevels[2]`, we can use the following method:

```
unlockedLevels.insert(3, atIndex: 2)
```

Now, our array of unlocked levels is ordered to `[1, 2, 3, 5, 8]`.

This is assuming though that we know a member of the array prior to 3 is sorted already. There are various sorting functionalities provided by Swift that could help keeping an array sorted. We will leave the details of sorting to our discussions of loops and control flow later in this chapter.

Removing items from an array is just simple. Let's again use our unlockedLevels array. Imagine that our game has an overworld for the player to travel to and from and the player has just unlocked a secret that triggered an event that blocked off access to level 1. Level 1 would now have to be removed from the unlocked levels. We can do it like this:

```
unlockedLevels.removeAtIndex(0) // array is now  [2, 3, 5, 8]
```

Alternately, imagine that the player has lost all of their lives and got a **Game Over** message. A penalty for this could be to lock the furthest level. Though probably a rather infuriating method and us knowing that level 8 is the furthest level in our array, we can remove it using the .removeLast() function of array types.

```
unlockedLevels.removeLast() // array is now [2,3,5]
```

 This is assuming that we know the exact order of the collection. Sets or dictionaries might be better at controlling certain aspects of your game.

Here are some ways to edit a set or a dictionary as a quick guide.

Set

```
inventory.insert("Power Ring")       //.insert() adds items to a set
inventory.remove("Magic Potion")      //.remove() removes a specific item
inventory.count                       //counts # of items in the Set
inventory.union(EnemyLoot)            //combines two Sets
inventory.removeAll()                 //removes everything from the Set
inventory.isEmpty                     //returns true
```

Dictionary

```
var inventory = [Float : String]() //creates a mutable dictionary

/*
one way to set an equipped weapon in a game; where 1.0 could
represent the first "item slot" that would be placeholder for
the player's "current weapon"
*/
```

```
inventory.updateValue("Broadsword", forKey: 1.0)


//removes an item from a Dictionary based on the key value
inventory.removeValueForKey("StatusBooster")

inventory.count                    //counts items in the Dictionary
inventory.removeAll(keepCapacity: false) //deletes the Dictionary
inventory.isEmpty                  //returns false

//creates an array of the Dictionary's values
let inventoryNames = [String](inventory.values)

//creates an array of the Dictionary's keys
let inventoryKeys = [String](inventory.keys)
```

Iterating through collection types

We can't discuss collection types without mentioning how to iterate through them en masse.

Here's some way we'd iterate though an array, a set, or a dictionary in Swift:

```
//(a) outputs every item through the entire collection
  //works for Arrays, Sets and Dictionaries but output will vary
for item in inventory {
    print(item)
}

//(b) outputs sorted item list using Swift's sorted() function
  //works for Sets
for item in sorted(inventory) {
    print("\(item)")
}

//(c) outputs every item as well as its current index
  //works for Arrays, Sets and Dictionaries
for (index, value) in enumerate(inventory) {
    print("Item \(index + 1): \(value)")
}

//(d)
//Iterate through and through the keys of a Dictionary
for itemCode in inventory.keys {
    print("Item code: \(itemCode)")
```

```
}

//(e)
//Iterate through and through the values of a Dictionary
for itemName in inventory.values {
    print("Item name: \(itemName)")
}
```

As stated previously, this is done with what's known as a for-loop; with these examples, we show how Swift utilizes the for-in variation using the `in` keyword. The code will repeat until it reaches the end of the collection in all of these examples. In example `(c)`, we also see the use of the Swift function, `enumerate()`. This function returns a compound value, `(index, value)`, for each item. This compound value is known as a tuple, and Swift's use of tuples makes for a wide variety of functionalities for functions, loops, as well as code blocks.

We will delve more into tuples, loops, and blocks later on.

Objective-C and Swift comparison

Here's a quick review of our Swift code with a comparison to the Objective-C equivalent.

Objective-C

Here's a sample code in Objective-C:

```
const int MAX_ENEMIES = 10;   //constant
float playerPower = 1.3;      //variable

//Array of NSStrings
NSArray * stageNames = @[@"Downtown Tokyo", @"Heaven Valley",
@" Nether"];

//Set of various NSObjects
NSSet *items = [NSSet setWithObjects: Weapons, Armor,
 HealingItems,"A", nil];

//Dictionary with an Int:String key:value
NSDictionary *inventory = [NSDictionary
dictionaryWithObjectsAndKeys:
            [NSNumber numberWithInt:1], @"Buster Sword",
            [NSNumber numberWithInt:43], @"Potion",
            [NSNumber numberWithInt:22], @"Strength",
nil];
```

Swift

Here's the equivalent code in Swift:

```
let MAX_ENEMIES = 10          //constant
var playerPower = 1.3         //variable

//Array of Strings
let stageNames : [String] = ["Downtown Tokyo","Heaven
Valley","Nether"]

//Set of various NSObjects
var items = Set([Weapons, Armor, HealingItems,"A"])

//Dictionary with an Int:String key:value
var playerInventory: [Int : String]  =  [1 : "Buster Sword",
43 : "Potion", 22: "StrengthBooster"]
```

In the preceding code, we used some examples of variables, constants, arrays, sets, and dictionaries. First, we see their Objective-C syntax and then the equivalent declarations using Swift's syntax. From this example, we can see how compact Swift is compared with Objective-C.

Characters and strings

For some time in this chapter, we've been mentioning strings. Strings are also a collection of data types, but a specially dealt collection of characters, of the class type, string. Swift is Unicode-compliant, so we can have strings like the following:

```
let gameOverText =   "Game Over!"
```

We can have strings with emoji characters like the following:

```
let cardSuits =   "♠ ♥ ♣ ♦"
```

What we did in the preceding code was create what's known as a string literal. A string literal is when we explicitly define a string around two quotes "".

We can create empty string variables for later use in our games such as:

```
var emptyString = ""               // empty string literal
var anotherEmptyString = String()  // using type initializer
```

Both are valid ways to create an empty string "".

String Interpolation

We can also create a string from a mixture of other data types, known as **String Interpolation**. String Interpolation is rather common in game development, debugging, and string use in general.

The most notable of examples are displaying the player's score and lives. This is how one of our example games, PikiPop, uses String Interpolation to display the current player stats:

```
//displays the player's current lives
var livesLabel = "x \(currentScene.player!.lives)"

//displays the player's current score
var scoreText = "Score: \(score)"
```

Take note of the `\(variable_name)` formatting. We've actually seen this before in our past code snippets. In the various `print()` outputs, we used this to display the variable, collection, and so on we wanted to get information on. In Swift, the way to output the value of a data type in a string is by using this formatting.

For those of us who came from Objective-C, it's the same as the following:

```
NSString *livesLabel = @"Lives: ";
int lives = 3;
NSString *livesText = [NSString stringWithFormat:@" %@
(%d days ago)", livesLabel, lives];
```

Note how Swift makes String Interpolation much cleaner and easier to read than its Objective-C predecessor.

Mutating strings

There are various ways to change strings, such as adding characters to a string as we did to collection objects. Here are some basic examples:

```
var gameText = "The player enters the stage"
gameText += " and quickly lost due to not leveling up"
/* gameText now says
"The player enters the stage and lost due to not leveling up" */
```

Since strings are essentially arrays of characters, like arrays, we can use the `+=` assignment operator to add to the previous string.

Also, akin to arrays, we can use the `append()` function to add a character to the end of a string.

```
let exclamationMark: Character = "!"
gameText.append(exclamationMark)
//gameText now says "The player enters the stage and lost due
to not leveling up!"
```

Here's how we iterate through the characters in a string, in Swift:

```
for character in "Start!" {
    print(character)
}
//outputs:
//S
//t
//a
//r
//t
//!
```

Note how again we use the for-in loop and even have the flexibility of using a string literal if we'd so like to be what's iterated through by the loop.

String indices

Another similarity between arrays and strings is the fact that a string's individual characters can be located via indices. Unlike arrays, however, since a character can be a varying size of data, broken in 21-bit numbers known as Unicode scalars, they can not be located in Swift with `Int` type index values.

Instead, we can use the `.startIndex` and `.endIndex` properties of a string and move one place ahead or one place behind the index with the `.successor()` and `.predecessor()` functions, respectively, to retrieve the needed character or characters of a string.

Here are some examples that use these properties and functions using our previous `gameText` string:

```
gameText[gameText.startIndex]               // = T
gameText[gameText.endIndex]                 // = !
gameText[gameText.startIndex.successor()]   // = h
gameText[gameText.endIndex.predecessor()]   // = p
```

There are many ways to manipulate, mix, remove, and retrieve various aspects of strings and characters. For more information, be sure to check out the official Swift documentation on characters and strings at `https://developer.apple.com/library/ios/documentation/Swift/Conceptual/Swift_Programming_Language/StringsAndCharacters.html`.

Commenting in Swift

In our code snippets thus far, one might note notations with double forward slashes `//` or with forward slashes and asterisks `/* */`. These are how we can comment or make notations in our Swift code. Anyone who's coded in C++, Java, Objective-C, JavaScript, or other languages will see that Swift works practically the same.

Single-line comments are started with the double forward slashes, `//`, while multiline comments or a comment block begins with `/*` and ends with `*/`.

Take the following example :

```
//This is a single line comment
/*
This is a comment block
that won't end until it reaches the closing
asterisk/forward slash characters
 */
```

Commenting is used to help navigate your code, understand what it might do, and comment out lines of code we might not want to execute, but at the same time want to keep for later (that is, `print()` log calls or alternative starting property values).

From Xcode 6 Beta 4 onward, we can also utilize the following comments: `// MARK:`, `// TODO:`, and `// FIXME`. `//MARK` is equivalent to Objective-C's `#pragma mark`, which allows the programmer to label a *section* of your code that is accessible in Xcode's top breadcrumb dropdown list. `// TODO:` and `// FIXME` give us the ability to section off parts of code that we wish to maybe add features to in the future or debug. Even games with well-organized class structuring can be daunting to sift through. The addition of these additional mark-up tools makes planning and searching through our games' code that much easier to do.

Boolean

An integral part of all programming, game, or otherwise is the use of **Boolean** values. Boolean values typically return either `true` or `false` values, `yes` or `no`, or `0` or `1`. In Swift, this is the job of the `Bool` class of objects. The use of the function `.isEmpty()` in our past collection data type examples returns a Boolean value of `true` or `false` based on whether that collection is empty or not.

In game development, one way we could use Boolean values is to have a global variable (a variable accessible in scope throughout our game/app) that checks if the game is over.

```
var isGameOver = false
```

This variable, taken from the PikiPop game, starts the game off with a variable of type `bool` named `isGameOver` with a starting value of `false`. If the events of the game cause this value to change to `true`, then this triggers the events associated with the game over state.

 Unlike Boolean values in Objective-C, Swift uses only `true` or `false` values to represent Boolean variables. *Swift strict type safety* does not allow the use of `YES` and `NO` or `0` and `1`, as we have seen in Objective-C and other programming languages.

However, reading and controlling this type of information about our game, known as the game's state, is best controlled with more than just a single Boolean value. This is because your game and the characters in your game could have various states, such as *game over*, *paused*, *spawn*, *idle*, *running*, *falling*, and more. A special object known as a *state machine* best manages this type of information. State machines shall be covered in more detail when we discuss the **GameplayKit** framework.

Ints, UInts, floats, and doubles

In addition to Boolean values, another basic data type we have up to this point briefly mentioned is the various numeric objects, such as integers (Ints), unsigned integers (UInts), floating point numbers / decimals (floats), and double precision floating point numbers / decimals (doubles).

Integers and unsigned integers

Integers represent negative and positive whole numbers, while unsigned integers represent positive whole numbers. Like with C and other programming languages, Swift lets us create various types of integers and unsigned integers from 8, 16, 32, and 64 bits. For example, an Int32 type is a 32-bit integer, while a UInt8 type is an 8-bit unsigned integer. The size of the bits for Ints and UInts represents how much space is being allocated to store the values. Using our UInt8 example, a number made from this type of unsigned Int can only store the values 0-255 (or 11111111 in a base-2 system). This is also known as 1 byte (8 bits). If we need to store numbers larger than 255 or negative numbers, then maybe an Int16 type would suffice as that can store numbers between –32767 and 32767. Usually, we don't have to worry too much about the size allocated by our integer variables and constants. So, using just the class name of Int will work fine in most cases.

The size of Int will differ depending on the type of system we are working on. If we are compiling our code on a 32-bit system, an integer will be equal to Int32, while the same integer would be an Int64 on a 64-bit system.

Swift can let us see what our minimum and maximum values are for an Int variable with the .min or .max class variables (that is, Int16.max = 32767 and UInt.min = 0).

Floats and doubles

Floats are 32bit floating point numbers / fractions, such as pi (3.14), or the golden ratio, phi (1.61803).

In game designing, we work with floating point values and ranges rather often, be it to determine the CGPoint in x and y of a 2D sprite, using linear interpolation for smoothing a game's camera movement in 3D space, or applying various physics forces on an object or 2D/3D vector. The precision needed for each situation will determine if a float is needed or if the 64-bit floating point value, the double is needed. Doubles can be as precise as 15 decimal places, while a float is six decimal places precise.

It's actually best practice to use doubles in situations that would work for either floats or doubles.

Objects in Swift

The core aspect of **object-oriented programming** (OOP) is of course the concept of objects. C++ began this paradigm in programming, while Java, C#, Apple's Objective-C, and other languages were all essentially built from this foundation.

Swift is an OOP language with the same dynamic object model as Objective-C, but presented in a cleaner, type-safe, and compact way.

You can think of an object exactly as it sounds, an abstract *thing* or *container*. An object can be something as simple as a string, or something as complex as the player object in the latest video game. Technically speaking, an object in a program is a *reference* to a set of various data in an allocated chunk of memory, but it's sufficient to just understand that an object can be a variable or a reference to an instance of a class, Struct, or block of code.

An object can have various data fields/aspects associated with it, such as properties, functions, parent objects, child objects, and protocols. In languages such as C for example, an integer variable is usually represented as just raw data, but the integer type in Swift is actually an object. Thus, we can access extra information and perform functions on Int objects in our code. We previously saw this with the Int.max variable, which returns the highest number that can be represented by the Int class. Again, depending on the machine you are working on, this could be the same value as Int32.max or Int64.max.

```
var highestIntNumber : Int = Int.max
```

Access to functions and properties of an object uses dot notation, as we saw with the previous example. Int.max and Int.min are actually special properties known as **class variables**, which represent all instances of an Int type object.

Let's look at how Swift deals with obtaining properties and functions of an instance of an object using a made-up Player type object.

```
let currentPlayer = Player(name:"Fumi")        // (a)
let playerName = currentPlayer.getName()       // (b)
var playerHealth = currentPlayer.health        // (c)
currentPlayer.attackEnemy()                    // (d)
```

We'll get back to the second half of line (a), but just understand that it creates an instance of an object of the type `Player` named `currentPlayer`. Line (c) creates a variable named `playerHealth` that's set by the `health` property of `currentPlayer`; here with the *dot notation*. Lines (b) and (d) use the dot notation to call the functions `getName()` and `attackEnemy()`. The `getName()` function in this case is a function that returns a string that's assigned to the constant, `playerName`. Line (c) creates a variable named `playerHealth` that is created by referencing the health property of `currentPlayer`, also using dot notation. Line (d) is a direct call to the `Player` class' `attackEnemy()` function, which you can imagine for now just performs what would make `currentPlayer` do her attack. This function doesn't return a value and thus is what's known as a `void` type function.

As for line (a), one might note that it doesn't use the dot notation. This is how Swift does what's known as a class initializer; designated by the parenthesis () after the class name and with the parameter called `name:` that sends a string, `Fumi`, to the object's class initializer.

We will be diving deeper in to the use of *objects* momentarily as we move on to functions and classes.

Type safety and type inference

Objects and, as we'll see, functions on these objects in Swift are type-safe. What this means is that if we perform a function on a string object when the code was expecting an integer, then the compiler will warn us early on in the process. In the vein of game design, if we were to have the player perform an action only an enemy supposed to do, then Swift will know through its inherently type-safe nature.

Swift's type inference is something we've mentioned before. Unlike other languages where you have to declare the object's type every time it's initialized, Swift will infer what type you mean. For example, we have the following:

```
var playerHealth = 100
//Swift automatically infers that playerHealth is an Int object
```

Optionals

As we stated before, Swift is a type-safe language. Apple also created Swift with the intention of keeping as many potential errors and bugs in the compilation state of development as opposed to runtime. Though Xcode has some great debugging tools, from the use of breaks, logging, and the LLDB debugger, runtime errors, particularly in games can be tough to spot, thus bringing the development process to a halt. To keep everything type-safe and as bug-free as possible during compilation, Swift deals with the concept of **optionals**.

Optionals, in short, are objects that potentially can be or start as nil. Nil, of course, is an object that has no reference.

In Objective-C, we could declare the following string variable for a game:

```
NSString *playerStatus = @"Poisoned";
playerStatus = nil;
```

In Swift, we would write this in the same way, but we'd find out very quickly that Xcode would give us a compiler error in doing so:

```
var playerStatus = "Poisoned"
playerStatus = nil      //error!
```

Even more confusing for anyone new to Swift, we'd also get an error if we did something as simple as this:

```
var playerStatus : String   //error
```

Creating empty/undeclared objects in our games makes sense and is something we'd often want to do at the start of our classes. We want that flexibility to assign a value later on based on the events of our game. Swift seems to be making such a basic concept impossible to do! No worries; Xcode will inform you in most cases to suffix a question mark, `?`, at the end of these `nil` objects. This is how you declare an object as an optional.

So, if we want to plan our game's properties and objects in Swift, we can do the following:

```
var playerStatus : String?  //optional String
var stageBoss : Boss?       //optional Boss object
```

Unwrapping optionals

Let's imagine that we want to display what caused a player to lose in the game.

```
var causedGameOver:String? = whatKilledPlayer(enemy.recentAttack)
let text = "Player Lost Because: "
let gameOverMessage = text + causedGameOver  //error
```

Because the string `causedGameOver` is optional, Xcode will give us a compile error because we didn't unwrap the optional. To unwrap the value in an optional, we suffix an exclamation point ! at the end of the optional.

Here's our `Game Over` message code, now fixed using the unwrapped optional:

```
var causedGameOver:String? = whatKilledPlayer(enemy.recentAttack)
let text = "Player Lost Because: "
let gameOverMessage = text + causedGameOver!  //code now compiles!
```

We can also force unwrap optionals early at declaration to allow any potential errors to be taken care of at runtime instead of when compiling. This happens often with @ `IBOutlets` and `@IBActions` (objects and functions linked to various storyboards and other tools that are based on menu/view tools).

```
@IBOutlet var titleLabel: UILabel!      //label from a Storyboard
var someUnwrappedOptional : GameObject! //our own unwrapped
optional
```

If possible, though it's recommended to use the basic wrapped optional ? as much as possible to allow the compiler to find any potential errors. Using what's known as optional binding and chaining, we can do some great early logic checks on optionals that in prior languages would have involved various `if` statements / control flow statements to simply check for nil objects.

Keeping code clean, safe, and easy to read is what Swift aims to do and why Swift goes out of its way sometimes to force many of these rules with optionals.

Optional binding and chaining

Optional binding is checking whether an optional has a value or not. This is done using the very handy if-let or if-var statements. Let's look back at our earlier code:

```
var causedGameOver:String? = whatKilledPlayer(enemy.recentAttack)
let text = "Player Lost Because: "
if let gotCauseOfDeath = causedGameOver {
    let gameOverMessage = text + gotCauseOfDeath
}
```

The code block, `if let gotCauseOfDeath = causedGameOver{...}`, does two things. First, using the key words, `if let`, it automatically creates a constant named `gotCauseOfDeath` and then binds it to the optional `causedGameOver`. This simultaneously checks whether `causedGameOver` is `nil` or has a value. If it's not nil, then the `if` statement's code block will run; in this case, creating the constant `gameOverMessage` that combines the `text` constant with `gotCauseOfDeath`.

We can use if-var to simplify this even further:

```
let text = "Player Lost Because: "
if var causedGameOver = whatKilledPlayer(enemy.recentAttack) {
    let message = text + causedGameOver
}
```

The if-var statement creates a temporary variable using our previously used optional `causedGameOver` and does a Boolean logic check based on the result of `whatKilledPlayer(enemy.recentAttack)`. The statement is true if there's a non-nil value returned. Note how we don't have to use either wrapped (?) or forced unwrapping (!) of the optional in such a case.

Optional chaining is when we query down into the properties of an object using the dot operator while also doing a nil/value check as we did with optional binding. For example, let's say that we have a game where certain Enemy types can cause a player to lose instantly via an Enemy instance named `currentEnemy`. In this example, `currentEnemy.type` would be a string that returns the name of the kind of enemy that hit the player. Optional chaining uses the custom dot modifier `?.` while accessing a potentially nil check on a property. Here's the code to get a better idea of how this works:

```
if let enemyType = currentEnemy?.type {
    if enemyType == "OneHitKill"
    {
        player.loseLife()  //run the player's lost 1
    }
}
```

Chances are that we'd probably not make an enemy without a designated type, but for the sake of understanding optional chaining, observe how this checks for the possible nil object that'd be returned by `currentEnemy.type` using `currentEnemy?.type`. Like how the dot operator functions where you can drill down the properties and properties of properties, the same can be done with the recurring `?.per` property that is drilled down. In this code, we do a Boolean comparison with `==` to see if `enemyType` is the string `OneHitKill`.

Don't worry if the syntax of the `if` statement syntax is a bit of a mystery; next, we discuss how Swift uses `if` statements, loops, and other ways we can control various object data and their functions.

Control flow in Swift

Control flow in any program is simply the order of instructions and logic in your code. Swift, like any other programming language, uses various statements and blocks of code to loop, change, and/or iterate through your objects and data. This includes blocks of code such as `if` statements, for-loops, do-while loops and Switch statements. These are contained within functions, which make up larger structures like classes.

If statements

Before we move on to how Swift handles one of the main topics of OOP, functions and classes, let's quickly run through if-else statements. An `if` statement checks whether a Boolean statement is `true` or `false`. We have the example as follows:

```
if player.health <= 0{
    gameOver()
}
```

This checks whether or not the player's health is less than or equal to `0`, designated by the `<=` operator. Note that Swift is OK with there not being parenthesis, but we can use this if we wish or if the statement gets more complicated, as in this example:

```
if (player.health <=0) && (player.lives <=0){ //&& = "and"
    gameOver()
}
```

Here, we check not just whether the player has lost all of their health, but also if all of their lives are gone with the and (`&&`) operator. In Swift, like in other languages, we separate out the individual Boolean checks with parentheses, and like other languages, we do a logic-or check with two bar keys (`||`).

Here are some more ways to write `if` statements in Swift with the added key words, else-if and else, as well as how Swift can check if-not a certain statement:

```
//(a)
if !didPlayerWin { stageLost() }

//(b)
if didPlayerWin
{
    stageWon()
}
else
{
   stageLost()
}

//(c)
if (enemy == Enemy.angelType){enemy.aura = angelEffects}
else if(enemy == Enemy.demonType){enemy.aura = demonEffects}
else{ enemy.aura = normalEffects }

//(d)
if let onlinePlayerID = onlineConnection()?.packetID?.playerID
{
   print("Connected PlayerID: /(onlinePlayerID)"
}

//(e)
if let attack = player.attackType, power = player.power where
power != 0 {
    hitEnemy(attack, power)
}

//(f)
let playerPower = basePower + (isPoweredUp ? 250 : 50)
```

Let's look at what we put in the code:

- (a): This checks the not / reverse of a statement with the exclamation point, `!`, via `!statement`.
- (b): This checks whether the player has won or not. Otherwise, the `stageLost()` function is called, using the key word `else`.

- (c): This checks if an enemy is an angel and sets its aura effect accordingly. If this is not, then it will check if it's a demon using else-if, and if that's not the case, then we catch all other instances with the `else` statement. We could have a number of else-if statements one after another, but if we start to stack too many, then using for-loops and Switch statements would be a better approach.

- (d): Using optional chaining, we create an `onlineID` constant based on `if`; we are able to get a non-nil `playerID` property using if-let.

- (e): This uses if-let, where optional binding became a feature in Swift 1.2. Instead of having nested if-lets and other logic checks, akin to how SQL queries are done in backend web development, we can create very compact, powerful early logic checking. In the case of example (e), we have an enemy receive an attack based on what type of attack it is and the power of the player.

- (f): This is an example of combining the creation of a constant with the keyword `let` and doing a shorthand version of an `if` statement. We shorten an `if` statement in Swift with the question mark ? and colon :. Here is the format for short handing an `if` statement: `bool ? trueResult : falseResult`. If `isPoweredUp` is `true`, then `playerPower` will equal `basepower + 250`; if `false`, then it's `basepower + 50`.

For loops

We touched on for-in loops before dealing with collections. Here again is a for-in loop in Swift that will iterate through a collection object:

```
for itemName in inventory.values {
    print("Item name: \(itemName)")
}
```

For some of us programmers who are used to the older way of using for-loops, don't worry, Swift lets us write for-loops in the C-style, which many of us are probably used to:

```
for var index = 0; index < 3; ++index {
    print("index is \(index)")
}
```

Here's another way of using a for-loop without using an index variable, noted with the underscore character _ but of course using a `Range<Int>` object type to determine how many times the for-loop iterates:

```
let limit = 10
var someNumber = 1
for _ in 1...limit {
    someNumber *= 2
}
```

Note the ... between the 1 and `limit`. This means that this for-in loop will iterate from 1-10. If we wanted it to iterate from 0 to `limit-1` (similar to iterating between the bounds of an array's index), we could have instead typed `0..<limit` where `limit` is equal to the array's `.count` property.

Do-while loops

Another very common iteration loop in programming is the do-while loop. Many times we can just utilize the while portion of this logic, so let's look into how and why we might use a while loop:

```
let score = player.score
var scoreCountNum = 0
while scoreCountNum < score {
    HUD.scoreText = String(scoreCountNum)
    scoreCountNum = scoreCountNum * 2
}
```

In game development, one use of the while loop (though executed differently in a game app, this accommodates iterating once per frame) is for displaying the counting up of a player's score from 0 to the score the player reached—a common esthetic of many games at the end of a stage. This while loop will iterate until it reaches the player's score, displaying on HUD object showing the intermediate values up until that score.

A do-while loop is practically the same as the while-loop with the extra caveat of iterating through the code block at least once. The end-stage score count example can also illustrate why we would need such a loop. For example, let's imagine that the player did really bad and got no score when the stage ended. In the while loop given, a score of zero won't let us enter the block of code in the while loop since it doesn't fulfill the logic check of `scoreCountNum < score`. In the while loop, we also have code that displays the score text. Though maybe embarrassing to the player, we would want to count up to the score and more importantly, still display a score. Here's the same code done with a do-while loop:

```
let score = player.score
var scoreCountNum = 0
```

```
do {
    HUD.scoreText = String(scoreCountNum)
    scoreCountNum = scoreCountNum * 2
} while scoreCountNum < score
```

Now score text will display even if the player scored nothing.

Switch statements

Switch statements are useful when we wish to check many different conditions of an object in a fully encompassing and neat way without having a wall of else-if statements. Here's a code snippet from the game PikiPop that uses a Switch statement from the game, PikiPop, that sets the percentage a GameCenter achievement (in this case, a 6x combo) based on the number of times the combo was achieved by the player. Don't worry too much about the GameCenter code (used with the GCHelper singleton object); that's something we will go over in future chapters when we make games in SpriteKit and SceneKit.

```
switch (comboX6_counter) {

        case 2:
            GCHelper.sharedInstance.
            reportAchievementIdentifier("Piki_ComboX6",
            percent: 25)
            break

        case 5:
            GCHelper.sharedInstance.
            reportAchievementIdentifier("Piki_ComboX6",
            percent: 50)
            break

        case 10:
            GCHelper.sharedInstance.
            reportAchievementIdentifier("Piki_ComboX6",
            percent: 100)

        default:
            break

    }
```

The switch statement here takes the variable used to count how many times the player hit a 6X combo, `comboX6_counter`, and performs different tasks based on the value of `comboX6_counter`. For example, when the player has done a 6X Combo twice, the Piki_ComboX6 achievement gets 25% fulfilled. The player gets the achievement (when at 100%) when the counter hits 10. The purpose of the keyword `break` is to tell the loop to exit at that point; otherwise, the next case block will iterate. Sometimes, this might be desired by your game's logic, but keep in mind that Swift, like many other languages, will continue through the switch statement without `break`. The keyword `default` is the catch-all block and is called when the value of the item checked by the switch statement is anything but the various cases. It can be thought of as an equivalent to the `else{}` block, while all of the cases are similar to `else if(){}`. The difference though is that Swift requires all cases of the switch be handled. So, though we can suffice with an `if` without an `else`, we have to have a default case for a switch statement. Again, this is done to keep Swift code safe and clean earlier in the coding process.

Functions and classes

Up until this point, we have kept from discussing probably the most important aspects of Swift or any OOP languages for that matter—how the language handles functions on objects and how it organizes these objects, object properties, and functions and performs various object-oriented design concepts, such as polymorphism and inheritance with classes, Structs, enums, protocols, and other data structures. There is much more to discuss about how Swift utilizes these concepts, more than we can fit in this chapter but throughout the course of this book, especially as we get into how to use
Apple's game-centric SpriteKit and SceneKit frameworks, we will flesh out more on these topics.

Functions

In Objective-C, functions are written the following way:

```
-(int) getPlayerHealth() {
    return player.health;
}
```

This is a simple function that returns the player's health as an integer—the `Int` equivalent in Objective-C.

The structure of the function/method is as follows in Objective-C:

```
- (return_type) method_name:( argumentType1 )argumentName1
joiningArgument2:( argumentType2 )argumentName2 ...
joiningArgumentN:( argumentTypeN )argumentNameN
{
  function body
}
```

Here's the same function in Swift:

```
func getPlayerHealth() -> Int {
    return player.health
}
//How we'd use the function
var currentHealth : Int = 0
currentHealth = getPlayerHealth()
```

This is how a function is structured in Swift:

```
func function_name(argumentName1 : argumentType1, argumentName2 :
argumentType2, argumentNameN : argumentTypeN) -> return_type
{
  function body
}
```

Note how we use the keyword `func` to create a function and how the argument/parameter names are first with the types second, separated by the colon (`:`) and within parenthesis.

Here's what a typical void function looks like in Swift. A void-type function is a function that doesn't return a value.

```
//with a Player type as a parameter
func displayPlayerName (player:Player){
    print(player.name)
}


//without any parameters; using a class property
func displayPlayerName(){
    print(currentPlayer.name)
}
```

In a void function, there's no need to write `->returnType`, but even if there are no parameters, we do have to put in the `()` parenthesis at the end of the function name.

Tuples

A rather powerful aspect of Swift is that function return types (and constants/ variables) can include a combination of values into a single value. These combinations are called **tuples**. Here's an example of an unnamed tuple:

```
let http503Error = (503, "Service Unavailable")
```

Here's a tuple used as a return type in a function direct from Apple's Swift documentation. Observe how it uses much of what we've learned thus far:

```
func minMax(array: [Int]) -> (min: Int, max: Int) {
    var currentMin = array[0]
    var currentMax = array[0]
    for value in array[1..<array.count] {
        if value < currentMin {
            currentMin = value
        } else if value > currentMax {
            currentMax = value
        }
    }
    return (currentMin, currentMax)
}
Excerpt From: Apple Inc. "IOS Developer Library".
https://developer.apple.com/library/ios/documentation
/Swift/Conceptual/Swift_Programming_Language/
Functions.html#//apple_ref/doc/uid/TP40014097-CH10-ID164
```

Classes

In OOP, classes make up the basic frame of an object, its functionality and interactions with other classes, objects, and various data structures, such as protocols, Structs, extensions, generics, and enumerations. In the following chapters, as we begin to structure our games, we will dive deeper into all of these concepts, but for now, let's understand the basics of classes and how they differ in Swift from Objective-C and other languages.

Here's the basic structure of a class in Swift:

```
//(a)
Global-project wide properties/variables
//(b)
class className : parentClassName, protocolName…protocolnName
{
//(c)
  class scope properties
//(d)
initializers (init(), convenience, required, etc)

//(e)
  func function_name1(argumentName1 : argumentType1,
  argumentName2 :    argumentType2, argumentNameN :
  argumentTypeN) -> return_type
  {
    function-scope variables and body
  }
                    .
                    .
                    .
  func function_nameN(argumentName1 : argumentType1,
  argumentName2 :    argumentType2, argumentNameN :
  argumentTypeN) -> return_type
  {
    function-scope variables and body
  }
//(f)
deinit()

} // end of the class
//(g)
global-project wide properties/variables (alternative position)
```

The Swift class structure works somewhat similar to what we see in C# and Java, as opposed to Objective-C's two files' (.h/header, .m/.mm/ implementation) setup:

- (a): We can have properties (like variables, constants, Structs, and enums) outside of the class declaration, which would make them global in scope, aka accessible throughout the entire project/game/app.

- (b): This is the actual class represented by what we named our .swift file. Again, this is different from Objective-C's classname.h - classname.m/.mm dual file setup for a single class. A class can be a child class of another class. We don't have to declare a parent/base class in Swift. Classes we make can be their own base classes. We can make classes as Objective-C classes by subclassing them from NSObject. The benefit of that is getting Objective-C runtime metadata and capabilities, but we take a hit in performance from the extra *baggage*. Either in the same place as the parentClass or after the colon : of parentClass, we can declare which protocols this class will adhere to. We'll discuss more on protocols later in the book, but just think of them as making sure your class utilizes the same functions as the protocol dictates.

- (c): These are where we'd place variables, constants, Structs, enums, and objects that are relevant for use in the scope of the class.

- (d): Initializers are special functions we use to set up the properties in section (c) when other classes and data structures use instances of the class via className(initializer parameters). We will discuss more on initializers more in the next chapter as we structure our games. They don't have to be at the top of the class, but it's a good practice to do so.

- (e): These are where your class functions will be declared and developed. We can have functions that are known as class functions. These are designated with the keywords class func. In short, class functions are part of the class as a whole as opposed to an instance of the class. It's best practice to place these above the next, more common type of function, the public functions, that can be accessed by other classes and properties via the dot operator (that is, className.function(parameters)). Using the private func keywords, as in C# and Java, we can create private functions that are only accessible to the class's own functions and properties.

- (f): The deinit() function is a special optional function that deals with how we clean up the data allocated by our class with memory management and eliminating what's known as memory leaks. Apple's **ARC** (**Automated Reference Counting**) handles most of this, but there are key words, such as weak and unowned, that we will at times have to put before various properties to make sure that they don't hang around after use.

    This is a rather involved topic, but worth looking into to avoid memory leaks in your game. ARC does take care of most of this, but there might be objects in your game that could potentially hang around. It's highly recommended to read Apple's own documentation on this topic, as memory management in iOS is always in the evolving stage. You can view the full documentation on ARC and memory management in Swift at `https://developer.apple.com/library/ios/documentation/Swift/Conceptual/Swift_Programming_Language/AutomaticReferenceCounting.html`.

- (g): If we wish, we can have global properties also at the bottom of our .swift files, after the end of the class declaration. Apple's own game example, Adventure (`https://developer.apple.com/library/ios/documentation/GraphicsAnimation/Conceptual/CodeExplainedAdventure/AdventureArchitecture/AdventureArchitecture.html#//apple_ref/doc/uid/TP40013140-CH2-SW5`), places global properties in this spot.

Summary

There's much more about the Swift programming language than we could fit here. Throughout the course of this book, we will throw in a few extra tidbits and nuances about Swift as it becomes relevant to our upcoming gaming programming needs.

If you wish to become more versed in the Swift programming language, Apple actually provides a wonderful tool in what's known as a **Playground**.

Playgrounds were introduced with the Swift programming language at *WWDC14* in June of 2014 and allow us to test various code outputs and syntaxes without having to create a project, build it, and run it and repeat again, when in many cases we simply needed to tweak a few variables and function loop iterations.

There are a number of resources to check out on the official Swift developer page (`https://developer.apple.com/swift/resources/`).

Two highly recommended Playgrounds to check out are as follows:

- **The Guided Tour Playground** (`https://developer.apple.com/library/ios/documentation/Swift/Conceptual/Swift_Programming_Language/GuidedTour.playground.zip`): This Playground covers many of the topics we mentioned in this chapter and more, from **Hello World** all the way to **Generics**.

- **The Balloons Playground** (`https://developer.apple.com/swift/blog/downloads/Balloons.zip`): The Balloons Playground was the keynote Playgrounds demonstration from *WWDC14* and shows off many of the features Playgrounds have to offer, particularly to make and test games.

Sometimes, the best way to learn a programming language is to test live code, and that's exactly what Playgrounds allow us to do.

In addition to testing snippets of code in our games, iOS 9 also allows us to plan and structure our games, which is the topic of the next chapter.

2
Structuring and Planning a Game Using iOS 9 Storyboards and Segues

Video game development has had an interesting history. It started as an offshoot of both electrical engineering and computer science. Games were a great challenge for engineers to make the most out of the limited hardware and, of course, make something fun. Today, video games and video game development are still built on those foundations of technology, math, and engineering but, for decades, have also been major players in the world of entertainment, storytelling, and media.

Be it if you are a major studio, a small team, or creating games all by yourself, planning and structuring your game projects can give you the foundation needed to save time in the development process, divide the work out to others if on a team, and of course, bring your game to life as close as possible to how you imagined it.

Starting with iOS 5, Apple took a page from the entertainment industry in how to structure and plan a project, big or small; by using the concept of storyboards. Storyboards are a graphic representation of the various steps and structures of a project; be it an animation, a movie, or in our case, iOS games. Storyboards will graphically show the flow of a production or app. In animation, for example, storyboards are used to flesh out major frames or story points of the production. Once it's agreed on as to what the series of events in a scene will be, animators will animate around those key points. Depending on whether the production is prelay or ADR, voice acting could also be placed into the storyboard process, which gives the animators even more specific content to work with.

In the case of the actual game application, storyboards can represent major parts of your game, such as the Intro scene, Opening Menu screen, Pause Screen, Game Over Screen, or the generic look of a main game level. Apple named these structures in Xcode **storyboards**, and the paths between them are known as **segues**. Throughout this chapter, we shall be looking into how to make use of these features while making a game app.

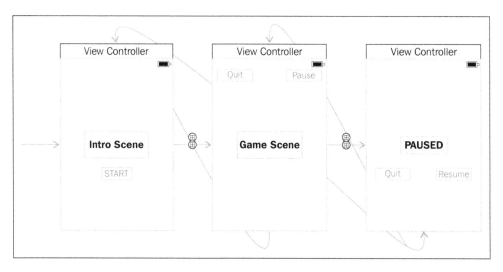

The preceding is an example of a simple iOS Storyboard.

Model-View-Controller

Before we get into storyboards in iOS 9, it's best that we first discuss the basic flow of an iOS app and the concept of **Model-View-Controller** (**MVC**). Model-View-Controller is an architectural paradigm used in software engineering, programming, and even now in web design. We can think of the model portion of MVC as the logic or *brains* of an application's behavior. This logic is usually independent of the user interface and determines what to do with the app's data.

We've actually already gone over the model portion of MVC! The Swift programming language discussed in the previous chapter is that model; this is the case with its Objective-C predecessor and any other programming language used in iOS or any other game development. Your game's code controls what to do with the player, level, and enemy/goal data.

The view portion of MVC is the visual representation of the model. This of course would include the numerous visual aspects of our games, from our player's animation frames, various in-game stats on the HUD, particle effects, and more.

The controller portion of MVC can be thought of as the *glue* that holds the model and view together. It is also the point at which the user of your game interacts with. Be it actions, such as a button press, a basic touch, a swipe, or other gestures, recognized by your iOS device, the controller takes that user input, manipulates your model and then the model updates your view accordingly.

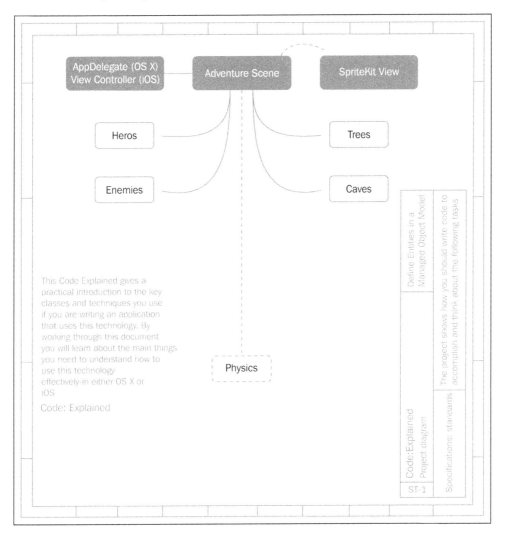

This diagram is taken from Apple's own Adventure Game Example.

When we work with iOS apps, the first recommended entry point for code and storyboard info is the Root View Controller. As we'll come to find out, MVC is intrinsically built into iOS app development and the Xcode IDE. Storyboards are a collection of different types of view controllers with varying tasks that are linked by segues.

An iOS app's lifecycle

Before we move on to working with storyboards, segues, and the foundation of our game apps, it's best we go over the overall lifecycle of an iOS app as it's important to know the entry points of our code and various objects/structures of our apps.

Insert app lifecycle imagery here before we move on to working with storyboards, segues, and the foundation of our game apps. It's best we go over the overall lifecycle of an iOS app as it's important to know the entry points of our code and various objects/structures of our apps.

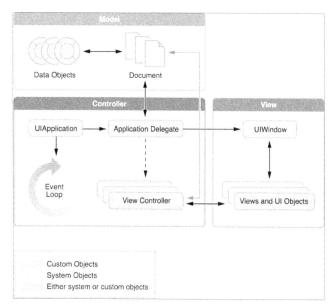

Source: https://developer.apple.com/library/ios/documentation/iPhone/Conceptual/
iPhoneOSProgrammingGuide/TheAppLifeCycle/TheAppLifeCycle.html

Anyone who has worked with C/C++, Java, or other languages will be familiar with the `main()` function. The `main()` function is used to designate your program's main entry point. The preceding example is how Apple designates the typical main function for apps. Essentially what this is doing is calling the first class in the typical lifecycle of iOS apps, the `AppDelegate` class.

The main() function

Here's the code with the `main()` function:

```
#import <UIKit/UIKit.h>
#import "AppDelegate.h"

int main(int argc, char * argv[])
{
    @autoreleasepool {
        return UIApplicationMain(argc, argv, nil,
        NSStringFromClass([AppDelegate class]));
    }
}
//Objective-C example of the Main() function
```

Note how the `main()` function is written in Objective-C. Swift again makes declaring the entry of your application easier.

```
@UIApplicationMain
class firstClassCalled
{
  //class code
}
```

While building an iOS app with Swift, the `main.m` file seen in prior Objective-C projects is no longer needed. Instead, we use an Attribute call, `@UIApplicationMain`, just before the declaration of the class that is first called.

Swift attributes

Attributes, beginning with the *at* character, @, are used to add additional information to a declaration or a type. In Swift, they have the following syntax:

```
@attribute name
@attribute name(attribute arguments)
```

As in other programming languages, attributes, depending on their functionality, can be used to describe objects, functions, and even entire classes.

For example, the @objc attribute is used to declare code that is readable in Objective-C.

As we'll see while using and linking various objects in the storyboards with our code, the attributes @IBOutlet and @IBAction are used to describe objects and functions representing objects we create in Xcode's Interface Builder.

We will discuss more on Attributes in *Chapter 7, Publishing Our iOS 9.0 Game*.

The UIApplication class/object

UIApplication is the object responsible for controlling an app's event-loop as well as handling other upper-level app processes. Game app or not, this is present in all iOS apps and is what is first called at the main entry point and works together with the AppDelegate class. Though it is possible to subclass UIApplication, it's usually not recommended. Customizations to what your game does during various app states are what we use the AppDelegate class and ViewControllers for, even if storyboards are not utilized (that is if you choose to mostly hardcode your game).

The AppDelegate class

We can think of the AppDelegate class as your app's main hub. It's the top level of general customization for your game. While making an app in Swift (game or not), it's the class that is given the @UIApplicationMain attribute because it's the general first entry of your game's model/code.

Here's the code that Apple provides with almost every iOS app preset in Xcode:

```swift
import UIKit

@UIApplicationMain
class AppDelegate: UIResponder, UIApplicationDelegate {

    var window: UIWindow?

    func application(application: UIApplication,
    didFinishLaunchingWithOptions launchOptions:
    [NSObject: AnyObject]?) -> Bool {
        // Override point for customization after
        application launch.
        return true
    }
    func applicationWillResignActive(application: UIApplication) {
        // Sent when the application is about to move from active
        to inactive state. This can occur for certain types of
        temporary interruptions (such as an incoming phone call
        or SMS message) or when the user quits the application
        and it begins the transition to the background state.
        // Use this method to pause ongoing tasks, disable
        timers, and throttle down OpenGL ES frame rates. Games
        should use this method to pause the game.
    }


    func applicationDidEnterBackground(application: UIApplication) {
        // Use this method to release shared resources, save user
        data, invalidate timers, and store enough application
        state information to restore your application to its
        current state in case it is terminated later.
        // If your application supports background execution,
            this method is called instead of
            applicationWillTerminate: when the user quits.
    }


    func applicationWillEnterForeground(application:
    UIApplication) {
        // Called as part of the transition from the background
            to the inactive state; here you can undo many of the
            changes made on entering the background.
    }
```

```
func applicationDidBecomeActive(application: UIApplication) {
    // Restart any tasks that were paused (or not yet
        started) while the application was inactive. If the
        application was previously in the background,
        optionally refresh the user interface.
}

func applicationWillTerminate(application: UIApplication) {
    // Called when the application is about to terminate.
        Save data if appropriate. See also
        applicationDidEnterBackground:.
}
}
```

This is the direct code and comments (as of Xcode 6.4) that Apple provides for us when using the iOS 9 game preset. Before we dive into structuring our games with storyboards and the two main frameworks (SpriteKit and SceneKit), it's best to understand what happens in this class. Events that happen to your game app relating to the device, particularly those that are outside of the player's control, such as incoming phone calls, notifications, and the device shutting down due to low battery power, as well as those controlled by the player (that is pausing the game), are handled by this class. As we see, Apple already provides great instructions for what each function of this class does, so be sure to review them. We will come back to these as we create our games and handle those specific situations. Note that the `AppDelegate` class has an optional variable (meaning it can be nil) named window and is of the type, `UIWindow`. A `UIWindow` object is a child of `UIView` and can allocate various displays/objects that can be put into the view of the user. Technically, we can use objects of `UIWindow` and `UIView` in code directly to create the visuals of our game, but Apple provides more robust objects that handle both the user's interaction with the screen and view. These objects are what make up iOS storyboards; the ably named, `ViewControllers`.

View controllers

View controllers are probably one of the most vital structures of iOS development and are what storyboards are visually representing when designing them in Xcode's Interface Builder. In terms of their typical entry point order, it's MAIN --> `AppDelegate` --> `RootViewController` --> [calls to any additional `ViewControllers` instance].

When we create a new app project in Xcode, Apple will make a default Root View Controller named `ViewController` for us. Here's it's code:

```
import UIKit
class ViewController: UIViewController {
    override func viewDidLoad() {
        super.viewDidLoad()
        // Do any additional setup after loading
        the view, typically from a nib.
    }
    override func didReceiveMemoryWarning() {
        super.didReceiveMemoryWarning()
        // Dispose of any resources that can be recreated.
    }
}
```

This is the starter code given to us in Xcode with the default `ViewController`. `swift` class. As we see, it's a subclass of `UIViewController` and thus inherits all of its parent class's functions. One of them shown here is the function `viewDidLoad()`. In Swift, when we wish to override a function of a parent class, we use the keyword `override` before the function declaration. We also see that `super.viewDidLoad()` is called as well. What this does is call the parent's own version of this function before we add our own code/customizations and is recommended when using any of the functions of `UIViewController`. The `UIViewController` functions handle various view states; `viewDidLoad()` handles when the view is first loaded and is called once for the life of the `UIViewController` object during an app's lifecycle. If we want to call some code every time a view is seen, we can use the `viewDidAppear()` function of `UIViewController` instead.

Here's a visual representation of these view states.

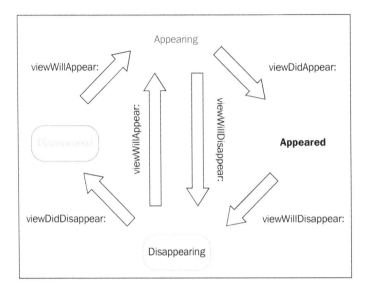

Here storyboards and segues, as we'll see, essentially give us a visual and customizable representation of these very states and the transitions between them without using too much code.

To dive even deeper into the `UIViewController` methods, check out Apple's documentation on the subject:

```
https://developer.apple.com/library/ios/documentation/UIKit/
Reference/UIViewController_Class/
```

For anyone familiar with the game development engine Unity (which has scripts written in either C#, JavaScript, or the Python derivative), one way we can imagine the `UIViewController` functions `viewDidLoad()` and `viewDidAppear()` is that they are somewhat similar to the Unity functions `Awake()` and `OnEnabled()`, respectively. One function is called when the scene is first loaded and the other just before the first frame that the object is visible/enabled. The `UIViewController` functions however are on a more upper-level basis for the entirety of the app as opposed to a per `gameObject` basis.

For more information and graphics on the entire iOS app lifecycle, check out the full documentation here:

```
https://developer.apple.com/library/ios/documentation/iPhone/
Conceptual/iPhoneOSProgrammingGuide/TheAppLifeCycle/TheAppLifeCycle.
html
```

View controller types

View controllers come in a number of types and we can create our own by subclassing them. The two main types are **container** view controller, which hold other view controllers, and content view controllers, which as we can imagine, are what display the content. Content view controllers include the `RootViewController`, which is the first view controller accessed after the app's entry point and is also the first view controller seen in the default `Main.Storyboard` file in a preset Xcode project's inspector. There are also other special types of view controllers, like the `UITableViewController`, used to display data listed in table cell formats and the `NavigationController`, which controls the navigation logic/ imagery of the app when moving between other view controllers.

For a more in-depth look at the various view controllers available in UIKit, check out the official documentation seen here:

```
https://developer.apple.com/library/ios/featuredarticles/
ViewControllerPGforiPhoneOS/index.html#//apple_ref/doc/uid/
TP40007457-CH2-SW1
```

It's actually at this point that we can begin to code our game, albeit entirely programming the MVC model. In the beginning of iOS game development, this was essentially how one would go about developing a game for the original iPhone. We'd programmatically work with the `UIWindow` and `ViewController` objects and our game's own custom classes to craft the app. As the family of iOS devices grew, an obvious issue began to arise. Though we can, and sometimes might have to. programmatically change code based on the device, dealing with a growing number of screen sizes and device types made it so that our code would always have to be refactored and produced ever increasing ambiguity whenever a new Apple iOS device was announced. Also, let's not forget that game development is as much of a visual designer / animator's work as it is a programmer's. Editing, positioning, refining, and later updating various visual aspects of a game can be very time consuming if done entirely via code.

Storyboards were made to help alleviate this issue by allowing us to visually design our game in the project itself as oppose to having our own possibly handwritten storyboards that describe just a model-based, code-centric design. With the introduction of Auto Layout in Xcode 5, we can, without using any code, make one project and general view for all varieties of iOS devices. We shall touch on AutoLayout as we now finally move on to working with Storyboards and segues, but for a more in-depth look on Auto Layout, check out the official documentation on Apple's developer portal: `https://developer.apple.com/library/ios/documentation/UserExperience/Conceptual/AutolayoutPG`.

Storyboards and segues

Let's now finally get to working with these tools and learn the basics of structuring game apps on a broader storyboard level. As of the writing of this book, the latest version of Xcode available is version 7.0. This will be the version we shall work with, but Xcode is always updating with even a beta version available to separately test the newest features.

Visit `https://developer.apple.com/xcode/` to download and read up on all that Xcode has to offer for iOS developers.

To start structuring your app using storyboards, follow these instructions:

1. First, open Xcode in your `Applications` folder (or in your Dock if you placed it there for easy access).

2. Next, click on **Create a new Xcode Project**.

3. You will now be asked to choose a template preset.

4. For the sake of just understanding storyboards and segues, select the Single View Application template. (Don't worry, we will be using the game template in the next chapter).

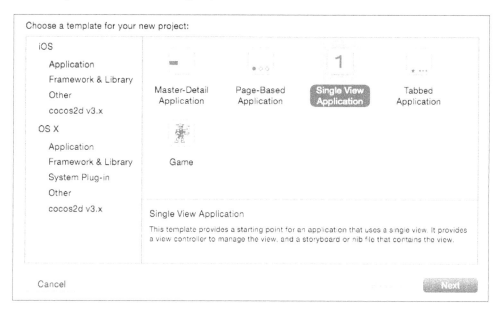

5. Now we choose our project's options. Name your project StoryBoardExample.

6. In the **Language** dropdown, make sure that it is set to **Swift** and ensure the **Devices** dropdown is set to **Universal**.

7. There should be other fields filled in by Xcode, such as your organization name and organization identifier. Those are involved with the information that will be published with your app when it comes to deployment as well as the content of your code's copyright comments. We can for now keep these at their default setting that Xcode has filled in.

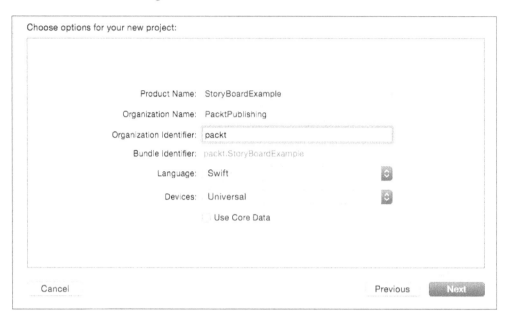

8. Click on **Next** and then select a valid location in your files to save this project.

Now we have our default app created by the template. We should see on the left-hand side, in the File Navigator Pane, various files and folders created for us. As we can see, the AppDelegate.swift and the ViewController.swift files were automatically created for us and right below that, we'd find the Main.Storyboard file. This is our storyboard and when you click on it, you should see the two panes open at the center of your Xcode window. The left side is the view controller **Scene** dropdown, which shows the hierarchy of the scene controlled by the provided the view controller. The right pane in the center allows us to visually see the view controller and eventually elements that we can place in it. The main visual part of the storyboard can be zoomed in and zoomed out. As we add more scenes to it, this will allow us to see the entirety of our storyboard or the portions we are working on.

You might have to zoom out slightly to see it (using your mouse or using the pinching gesture on your trackpad with a MacBook), but to the left of the View Controller scene there's a gray arrow. This is the entry point and the first View Controller scene attached to this arrow is your `RootViewController`/Initial scene.

When adding more scenes to your storyboard, for either debugging purposes or design choice, you can simply change the scene that is first entered by clicking and dragging that arrow to the left of that scene.

Let's start by creating a separate scene for our storyboard:

1. At the bottom of the **Utilities** panel (the far right panel of the Xcode project), there are four icons designating the various snippets and objects we can place in our project's code and the storyboard. Click on the third icon from the left if it's not already selected. This will open the Object Library.

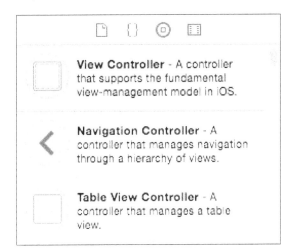

2. We can see that the very top of the Object Library has a **View Controller** object.

3. Drag this onto the storyboard's canvas, preferably to the right of the initial scene.

 If the **Utilities** panel isn't open, click on the upper right-most icon at the top of your project's toolbar window.

 The three buttons in your toolbar can be toggled to close the **Navigation** pane, **Debug** pane, and **Utilities** pane, respectively. Closing these when applicable can help expand the general view, known as the canvas of your storyboard scenes.

Now we have two scenes in our storyboard, but nothing is there to tell us what they are. They are just two blank scenes!

Let's put a **Label** object in these scenes to represent what they are and at runtime tell us which one we are in.

To keep this in the mindset of developing a game, let's put a label in the first one called **Intro Scene**, where we'd maybe have an intro animation to our game with a **Start/Options** menu, and in the next one, put the label Game Scene to represent that this is where that actual gameplay would occur.

Here's how to do that:

1. Go to the bottom of the **Utilities** panel and use the search field to search label. This will isolate the label object, so you don't have to scroll through the entire list.

2. Drag the `label` object to the canvas of the first scene. If it doesn't look like it's trying to snap to the scene's canvas, you might have to select the **View** portion of that view controller scene's hierarchy, using the left pane of the Main/Storyboard's main view. Alternately, you can also double-click the view in the Inspector to get the scene in focus so that you can place the label onto it.

3. As we drag it, try to center the label as best as possible. The canvas will indicate that we are at the vertical and/or horizontal part of that scene with dotted blue lines. Drop it in the center.

The **Utilities** pane should have some fields visible when selecting the label to control various aspects of its text like font size, alignment, and style.

4. The label will just say Label as the default, so let's rename it to Intro Scene for the first scene by either double-clicking the label itself in the canvas, or changing the name in the second field down from **Text** in the **Utilities** panel.

5. Let's make this label a bit more prominent, so single-click on the label, click on the [T] icon in the **Font** field, and make the style bold with a size of 28.

   Note how the label is clipped from the size increase and hardly visible.

6. Simply click on the label and expand out any one of the eight scaling icons at the corners of the label object on the canvas.

   Reposition the label to return it to the center of the scene.

7. Create the same label for the second scene we added by simply typing *Command + D* to duplicate the label (as to not have to repeat all of the steps) and then drag it to the center of the other scene. Zoom out as needed and possibly click back on to the view part of the hierarchy if the focus change prevents the ability to drag the label across.

Though rather rudimentary and with still some more work to do with, this is all it takes to create separate scenes visually. If you have an idea of how you want to structure your game, this is where you can start with the use of storyboards. Of course, there is still more to do here before we make this storyboard have any function.

We can see that Xcode is giving us the following warning:

Scene is unreachable due to lack of entry points and does not have an identifier for runtime access via `-instantiateViewControllerWithIdentifier`.

This is referring to the Game Scene object that is essentially orphaned due to no connection to the Intro Scene nor the app's entry point.

This is where segues come into play. Yet, before we work with segues and create a flow to these scenes and more, if we were to run this app, we'd note another issue. We could have sworn that we centered the text, but if simulating or running this in, say, an iPhone 6s, the text is completely off to the upper-right side. This is because the default canvas is a generalized *all device* template to begin with via Auto Layout.

Auto Layout has gotten easier with each new build of Xcode, but one could still argue it's still a bit of a hassle at times to fine tune, particularly when creating constraints (set spaces/margining between various storyboard objects). Let's take a quick look at how to work with constraints.

One quick way to alleviate the issue we have here is to just work with the **Base Values** panel found at the bottom center of the storyboard canvas by clicking on the **w/Any h/Any** text. Once clicked, a pop-up table of cells will appear. Rolling over with your mouse or trackpad to the various cells will bring up a number of different configurations as oppose to w/Any h/Any. What's great about this is that you can change/add and delete various objects simply based on the device type using these options.

Before storyboards and Auto Layout, this would involve huge amounts of testing and refactoring of code in a view controller or Nib classes to get the layout just the way you'd like visually. Apple would then create the next device with a different screen size to prior devices, it would become an even greater hassle or the developer would risk a broken game on the newest device.

To make the labels be in the center for all iPhones in portrait mode for example:

1. Hover and click on the center left-hand side of the Auto Layout panel where it'll say **Compact Width | Any Height** at the top of that pop-up panel/table.

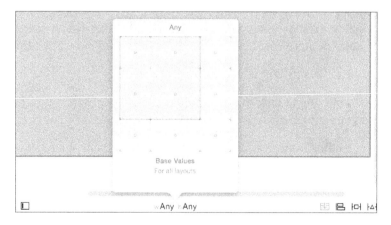

2. This should now change the display text at the bottom of the canvas to **w/Compact h/Any** and shrink the width of the scene as this layout represents all iPhones in Portrait and of any height (so it could be a bit off in height on an older iPhone 4S as oppose to the iPhone 5 or later).

3. Note how the labels are off center toward the upper right. This is what would have been seen in the simulator or on an actual iPhone in the portrait orientation. Drag them back to the center, and they should now look as they are seen in this configuration of the storyboard's canvas. If designing for iPad, then the other configurations would need to be changed for that.

Pinning with constraints could actually streamline this process. For example, let's say that you want to place a **Pause** button at the upper right corner of your Game Scene and you know that no matter the orientation, it will always be at a certain distance (in percentages or pixels) away from the right and top of a device's screen. We can click on the pin button at the bottom of the canvas to create these constraints in the **w/Any h/Any** configuration and skip manually adjusting the icon on every one of the base configurations.

Xcode already gives us a scene, the `LaunchScreen.xib` file, which, if you have already ran your code, was actually what was seen first before the first view controller in the storyboard.

To have just your `Main.Storyboard` file be at startup you can select the main project file at the top left corner in the **Navigation** pane and in the **Launch Screen** dropdown of the **Apps Icons and Launch Images** section, select `Main.Storyboard`. Then, you can delete the `LaunchScreen.xib` file if no longer needed. It can be a good file to see working constraints, and if so be it, it can be your initial splash screen for your game. More on constraints can be found here in the official documentation: `https://developer.apple.com/library/prerelease/ios/documentation/UserExperience/Conceptual/AutolayoutPG/WorkingwithConstraintsinInterfaceBuidler.html`.

Segues

Games have scenes, and all scenes have transitions between them. Segues are simply transitions between scenes in a storyboard. Segues come in various types:

- **Show**: This pushes the next view controller on top of the current one; it also allows for calling back if using a `UINavigationController` instance.

- **Show Detail**: When using `UISplitViewController`, a Container view controller is typically used in iPad apps to browse news/email apps, where the left side of the page is a `UITableViewController` object and the other side of the same page are the details of that table/list. This calls the details for the `DetailView` controller portion of the page when triggered by a gesture from the selected item on the `UITableViewController` side.

- **Present modally**: This presents the next view controller over the current but in such a way that it can be canceled, such as a full-page popup.

- **Popover**: This is like Present modally but with more options in sizing to create a smaller pop-up window that can be closed and disposed of.

- **Custom**: This is a version of a segue that you can completely customize with OOP code.

The typical storyboard structure when building say, an e-mail app, will more than likely need to make use of a navigation controller and UITableView controllers to structure the data and flow of the app. Now, we can very well do the same thing for game apps. Game Over, Menu, Rankings, and Pause screens could make use of these view controllers. For our example, we'll keep it simple and unrestricted to let you, the developer, have a better starting point to branch from.

 Our example here is rather simple, but in addition to providing code for this project, an even more detailed storyboard will be available using various view controllers and objects.

Let's take care of that warning and link up these scenes as well as begin to show the overall structure of a typical game using storyboards.

1. First, in the **Intro Scene**, place a button labeled **START** right under the **Intro Scene** label. Placing a button on a storyboard is done exactly the same as with a label. Search for button or scroll down the objects in the **Utilities** panel and then drag and drop the button onto the scene.

2. Now create two more buttons on the Game Scene view; one button labeled **Pause** at the top-right corner of the scene and another named **Quit** opposite the Pause button on the upper-left corner.

3. Create a new ViewController object on the scene, preferably above or below the Game Scene on the canvas.

4. On the new Pause Scene, create a label PAUSED the same way the Game Scene and Intro Scene labels were made.

5. Then, add two buttons, **Quit** and **Resume**, and place them right under the **PAUSED** label.

Now to create the segues visually using the storyboard:

1. Control-Click the **START** button object on the Intro Scene and then while still pressing Control-Click, drag the object toward the **Game Scene** on the canvas. You should see a blue line follow your cursor as you drag across. (if you need more space, zoom out a bit and also temporarily close the **Navigation** and **Utilities** panels using the toll bar buttons).

2. Drop this point anywhere on the view that isn't another object; you should see the entire view glow blue while doing so.

3. A popup asking for the type of Segue will come up. Select **Show**.

4. That's it! You've created a segue, and you've also told the storyboard that when the user clicks that button, it'll open the Game Scene — View Controller.

5. Before you move on to creating more segues, click on the door-like symbol on the canvas that represents the segue. On the top right in the **Utilities** panel's Assets inspector, you should see an empty **Identifier** field. We can leave the segue empty if we'd like, but naming it could be of use if we wish to call the segue in code with the following line:

```
performSegueWithIdentifier("segueIDNameeWithIdentifi)
```

6. Now repeat steps *1* through *3* to create the following segues:

    1. Link Game Scene's **Quit** button back to Intro Scene.
    2. Link Game Scene's **Pause** button to the PAUSED Scene.
    3. Link PAUSED Scene's **Resume** button to the Game Scene.
    4. Link PAUSED Scene's **Quit** button to the Intro Scene.

The warning should now be gone as all of the scenes are connected with segues, and after possibly some Auto Layout fixes, running the app now has a game-like scene structure that transition the way we'd normally see in other games. We can go from here and make other scenes, such as a Game Over scene, a Stage Win scene, or others. Even if this might not be the way you'd like your final game's transitions to end up (particularly since the default transition of the Show segue does a quick vertical), this can be a very quick way of prototyping your game right off the bat. Custom segues and segues triggered with code are how we can dive deeper into fine tuning when the default setting might not match with our vision of our games.

Here's more documentation on making custom segue classes if you really want to dive deeper into segues:

```
https://developer.apple.com/library/prerelease/ios/documentation/
UIKit/Reference/UIStoryboardSegue_Class/index.html#//apple_ref/doc/
uid/TP40010911-CH1-SW11
```

Similarly to how we Control-Dragged the button's linkage to the next view controller scene, we can do the same to our `ViewController.swift` file.

Here's a summery on how to do that for the first view controller:

1. Remove the previous segue. One way to do so is to right-click the button and to click on **x** in the **Triggered Segues** section.

2. Click on the Intro Scene's view in the hierarchy to get it in focus.

3. Control-Drag a blue line from the yellow icon on the top left of the Intro Scene's view controller to the Game Scene's view controller and select the Show type of segue.

4. Click on the segue icon in the canvas and now give the identifier of this segue the name `startGame`.

5. Open the Assistant Editor (the two interlocking circles button on the top-right portion of the Xcode toolbar); close some panes to make any needed room.

6. Control-Drag the **Start** button into the `ViewController` class; preferably at the bottom of the code but still within the class's closing brackets.

7. This will prompt the outlet/action popup. Select the **Action** option in the **Connection** dropdown and name it `startButton`.

8. This will create the `IBAction` function: `@IBAction func startButton(sender: AnyObject) {}`.

9. Type the following code between the braces: `self.performSegueWithIdentifier("startGame", sender: nil)`

10. This tells the view controller to perform the segue when this button is prompted using code.

Storyboards versus coding

There's no single correct way to do the design structure of your app as long as the MVC model is followed. Actually, there are programmers out there who are completely fine with just using the initial view controller and never use a single Nib or storyboard file; thus purely building their game controlled by the logic of their code and calls to the various View objects programmatically. In iOS development, there's somewhat of a design split between three main branches, hardcoding, Nibs, and storyboards. The original methodology was coding; Nibs came in later to first allow direct visual editing in Xcode and then that evolved into Storyboards, further built upon with the addition of Auto Layout.

The reason there's a split between some developers and studios on the visual structure methodology of an iOS app is because one drawback to Nibs and storyboards are their lack of portability. If you wanted to port your game to another platform, such as Android, at descent pace, heavy use of storyboards would make it a rather tough to port the app to the other platform since these design features are specific to the iOS platform. This is when pure code would be more beneficial. Storyboards though give us developers an editable, visual representation of the app/game we wish to make and the ability to do little to no changes as the family of devices change.

Even other game development engines, such as Unity, Unreal Engine, and more, work on a more sandboxing, visual representation methodology with your code acting as more of a component to the visual as opposed to the full structure of everything that appears before your game characters even get rendered to the screen.

Summary

In this chapter, we went over a number of app project structuring and introduction topics. First, we went over the Model-View-Controller paradigm followed by all apps, game or not, and the overall lifecycle of an iOS app that follows this structuring. Next, we reviewed the entry point(s) and pathway of your code in a typical app as well as the upper-level objects used along the way, such as the Application system object, the `AppDelegate` class, and view controller. Last but not least, we discussed the main topic of the chapter—storyboards, segues, and instructions on how to create a simple game flow structure. From here, we can see how relatively easy and quick it can be to structure various scenes for your game and transition between them with segues. Again, note that although storyboards are recommended, they can simply start as a general guide toward the final product, which gives you, the developer, the ability to visualize your game even if in the end preferring a more code-heavy design choice.

In the next two chapters, we are going to finally get into really coding and designing actual playable games. We will start off with 2D games, and since iOS 7, Apple has given iOS developers it's own framework to handle 2D sprites and game physics. This framework is amply named Spritekit.

3
SpriteKit and 2D Game Design

Now that we understand the basics of coding in Swift, the generic flow and class structure of an iOS app, as well as the optional structuring of apps with storyboards and segues, we can move on to transforming our apps into playable games.

For this chapter, we will begin with the 2D game design and game development framework created exclusively by Apple for iOS game developers known as SpriteKit. SpriteKit first became available with iOS 7 to help simplify the game development process for the family of iOS devices. The framework runs a typical rendering loop to draw and update 2D objects/sprites to your game's scene. There's much going on behind the scenes to run this loop and draw your game sprites. Thankfully, Apple built the first party game development frameworks to do much of the heavy lifting for us. This way, we can focus more on making the game itself without worrying too much about how that game will connect and run with the hardware, something developers in the past had to contend with.

Every update of iOS and Xcode continues to add more tools and frameworks to improve the ease of game design, including the companion framework introduced first at *WWDC15* for iOS 9 known as **GameplayKit**. GameplayKit can allow us to separate, copy, and modularize the game logic and even copy for use in future game projects, be it SpriteKit or the 3D framework of our next chapter, SceneKit. We will go over GameplayKit in later chapters as well. At the end of this chapter, we will look at a complete game example that is for a simple game in its gameplay but somewhat complex in its logic.

A brief history of iOS game development engines

SpriteKit and the 3D game framework, SceneKit, were not the first methods used for developing games in iOS. We'll quickly see why it became a welcomed addition to the developer toolset. Initially, we, the game developers, had to practically talk directly with the GPU using the OpenGL API to put both 2D and 3D graphics/ vertices on to the screen. On the upper level, there always was Foundation and CocoaTouch to interact with user gestures to manipulate UIKit objects, but dealing with game development essentials, such as SpriteSheets, mipmaps, normal maps, partial emitters, bounding boxes, and culling, involved some level of lower-level structuring. Apple made those calls to various graphics buffers and VBOs slightly easier when they created their GLKit framework in 2011. Thankfully, various third-party frameworks, such as Cocos2D, Box2D, Sparrow, GameMaker, Unity, Unreal Engine, and others made this process less engineering-intensive in an effort to keep the *design* aspect of game design the focus. GameMaker, Unity, and Unreal Engine are more sandboxing- / drag-and-drop-styled engines akin to the mentality behind storyboards and segues, while engines such as Cocos2D and Sparrow are more code-heavy / boilerplate OOP structures that shortcut the initial coding buildup. Engines such as Unity and Unreal Engine are great in that they offer a more hands-on sandboxing-type environment with various features that simplify the MVC model. Some drawbacks to such engines are that they are sometimes closed source, usually cost money to utilize to their fullest and aren't device-specific (Unity particularly falls into this category). Working with these visual engines could sometimes lead to optimizations being required in platform-specific IDEs such as Xcode, due to a sometimes *one-size-fits-all* methodology. Apple's SpriteKit and the 3D API, SceneKit which we'll see later, give us a first-party platform-specific middle ground that grants the developer both upper-level API editing, but even lower-level graphic API (OpenGL/Metal) customizations.

The negatives to sandbox/drag-and-drop-styled engines have decreased over time. Engines used by AAA studios, such as Unreal Engine, Unity, Havok, and others have lessened their upper-level ambiguity between the API and targeted devices' lower-level code. A good example of this would be Unity's IL2CPP, which converts the upper-level API calls directly to fast device-specific C++ code. This includes code and graphics pipeline optimizations that make use of Apple's slim Metal API. This homogenization of upper level applications with traditional boilerplate code now allows developers from all skill levels to make amazing games. That is why from iOS 8, iOS 9, and onwards, the Apple game development frameworks adopted a more visual design methodology. Xcode 7 introduced game state machines, components, and the ability to edit/copy and reuse player actions and animations throughout your projects. This allows developers to work specifically in iOS/Xcode while utilizing the visual design benefits of the device-independent game engines.

For this chapter, we will learn how to make a tile puzzle game named `SwiftSweeper` using the SpriteKit framework and with a more traditional boilerplate code method. This means that we will make our first demo game in a code-heavy / model-centric fashion. Not only will this give us a look into the inner workings of SpriteKit's code but it will also let us utilize more from the Swift programming language from *Chapter 1*, *The Swift Programming Language*.

We will conclude this chapter by briefly mentioning Apple's latest SpriteKit demo game, DemoBots, which utilizes more of the visual tools/frameworks from Xcode 7 and later. Seeing the more code-intensive method first though will later let us appreciate the time saved with these newer tools.

Apple has gone out of their way to mimic the visual design methodology to game design seen in other engines since game design is as much about code/logic as it is about art and design.

The game loop

The game loop is a game developer's roadmap. The names differ depending on the framework and platform, but the same rules apply. The game loop comprises of all the methods, physics updates, and draw calls that occur during a single frame of your game and their order of execution. The golden rule to game development is to try to keep this loop always spinning in full iterations at no slower than 16.6 milliseconds, or 60 frames per second.

There are aspects of the game loop that don't have to be controlled by the game developer as much as they used to be in the past, though we do have the option to work down to the very GPU calls using OpenGL, or even better, Apple's Metal API. We will discuss more on these topics later on.

Here is what the SpriteKit game loop looks like:

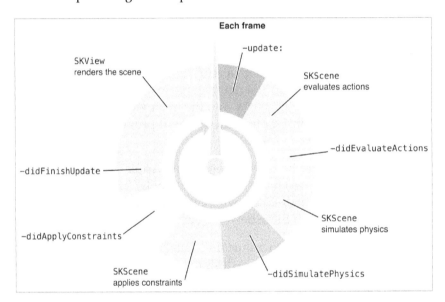

The preceding is an illustration given to us directly from the Apple Developer site. We see a number of functions that are called during a single frame. The first function iterated through is update(). The update() function is where we add most of our own game-specific updates and various checks on game objects (such as positions and character statuses).

The loop structure gives us the option to do updates after we know a certain set of tasks in the frame have happened, that's where `didEvaluateActions()`, `didSimulatePhysics()`, `didApplyConstraints()`, and `didFinishUpdate()` functions come in handy.

> Anyone coming from Unity might be familiar with its general game loop functions, such as `Awake()`, `Start()`, `FixedUpdate()`, `update()`, and `LateUpdate()`. The SpriteKit game loop allows some similar code/render flow, but as we'll see, there are some slight differences.
>
> For more on the game loop and its functions, see the following link from the Apple documentation at `https://developer.apple.com/library/ios/documentation/GraphicsAnimation/Conceptual/SpriteKit_PG/Actions/Actions.html`.

Utilizing the other game loop methods could make sure certain calls in your game don't go out of order and can even help with the important task of making the most out of each frame in a fast, efficient manner.

For instance, in the public game PikiPop, mentioned previously, here's how the game uses the game loop in its main `GameScene.swift` code:

```
//Update() Example
//From main GameScene.swift
override func update(currentTime: CFTimeInterval) {
        //Update player
        if(player?.isPlayable==true){
            player!.update(currentTime)
        }
    }
```

The preceding code first checks whether the player is playable with the `isPlayable` Boolean. This status can mean a number of things, like if the player is alive or not, is spawning, and so on. The game loop's `update()` function, which is being overridden from its parent `update()` function of the `SKScene` object, takes a parameter of the time utility type `CFTimeInterval`. `CFTimeInterval` is a special Core Foundation double type that measures time in seconds and thus updates the player object (if not null) during each interval.

As a brief summary of PikiPop, it's a procedural 2D side-scrolling game somewhat similar to the game Flappy Bird. Unlike Flappy Bird, Piki is able to traverse the game in all directions based on player taps and swipes. Piki could get trapped between the stage objects and the edge of the stage.

The preceding image is Piki getting injured if pushed into the left-hand side of the screen.

Edges in that game's stages use SpriteKit's own special objects named **SKConstraints**. More on these later, but in short, they dictate the range and orientation SpriteKit sprites can take. Sprites in SpriteKit (both developer-defined objects, such as PikiPop's Player object and the default SKSpriteNode) are all derived from SKNode objects that work with SKConstraints and other physics-based framework functionality.

We could check whether Piki is being pushed against the corner in the update() part of the game loop, but since constraints are part of the framework's physics architecture, it's best to do this check during the didSimulatePhysics() portion of the render loop of SKScene as seen here:

```
override func didSimulatePhysics() {

    //run check on Player
    let block: (SKNode!, UnsafeMutablePointer<ObjCBool>) ->
    Void  = { node, stop in
        /*checks if the node is the player and is moved/crushed
        to the left by a physics object.  This is done by
        comparing the node's position to a position that is,
        in this case, less than 26% off the left side of the
        screen; calculated by multiplying the screen's width
        by 0.26  */
```

```
      if let playerNode = node as? Player{
          if (playerNode.position.x < self.frame.size.
          width*0.26 && playerNode.isPlayable) {
              playerNode.playerHitEdge()
          }

      }

  }


      ...more code
```

The first part of this code, `let block: (SKNode!,`
`UnsafeMutablePointer<ObjCBool>) -> Void  = { node, stop in,` is done
in what's known as a **block** or a **closure** syntax, which Swift lets us do rather
dynamically. Don't mind the details of this kind of code for the moment; just note
that we check the player's position in *x* versus the edge of the window's frame in this
portion of the game loop.

Here's more information on writing blocks/closures in Swift:
`https://developer.apple.com/library/prerelease/ios/`
`documentation/Swift/Conceptual/Swift_Programming_`
`Language/Closures.html`

Tile game – SwiftSweeper

Time to stop talking about SpriteKit and get right into it! As stated at the beginning
of this chapter, we will first show you how to make a simple-looking tile game in
SpriteKit using the slightly more difficult boilerplate/code-drive-styled design. Don't
worry, this is not going to involve direct calls to the GPU with C++ and handling
extremely tiny memory requirements like veteran game developers did during
the early console days. However, we will be using lots of code-heavy calls with
SpriteKit objects, functions, and classes. Granted, getting down into the code directly
is continually becoming less of the developer's responsibility as Apple continues to
make more design-centric functionalities in Xcode.

Knowing the code structure can give you an edge over developers coming in on a more top-down methodology and coding will always be behind custom game logic.

What is SwiftSweeper?

SwiftSweeper is a clone of the classic tile puzzle game, MineSweeper, written entirely in Swift. SwiftSweeper makes use of Swift's ability to use Unicode emoticons so that we don't have to use many image assets and should give us a great starting point to making our own tile/puzzler game with difficulty levels.

We will build up much of the game from scratch, but the full source code can be found at https://github.com/princetrunks/SwiftSweeper.

 As at the time writing of this book, this was built in Xcode 7 Beta (7A120f) for the initial iOS 9 release and optimized for iPhone.

The goal of the game is to tap every tile on the game board without hitting mines hidden throughout the board. You do get some help though. Every tile that isn't a mine will tell the player how many tiles around it are mines. If the player knows that a tile without a doubt is a mine via the process of elimination, they can plant a flag on that tile to make sure that they don't tap that space. Tap all of the tiles that aren't a mine to win the game! SwiftSweeper even saves the time it took you to win for each difficulty level you chose to give the game a bit of replay value.

Creating our SpriteKit game

Now that we know the goal of our game, here's how we go about building it in SpriteKit:

1. First, open Xcode and create a new project.

2. Now select the Game template and click on **Next**.

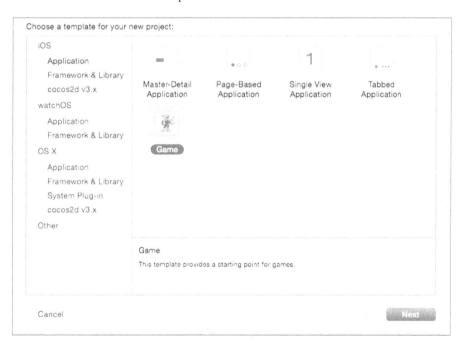

3. Next, fill in the product name. We will name this project `SwiftSweeperExample` and make sure that the language is Swift with **SpriteKit** selected as the game technology as well as the devices set to iPhone.

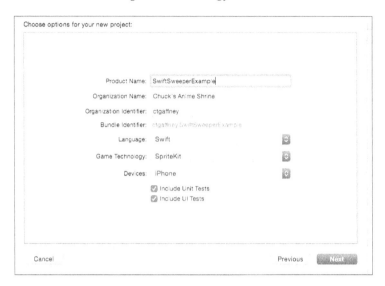

4. Then, click on **Next**, and we now have a brand new SpriteKit game project with a number of files already written up for us to get us started.

5. Now click on the project's main file in the navigation pane and deselect all but the **Portrait** selection in the **Device Orientation** field.

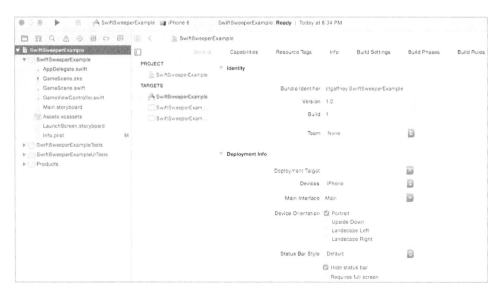

6. Since we are going to work mostly with code, we can also either ignore or delete the `GameScene.sks` file for now. These files are Xcode's option for you to visually design your game scene. We will know more on these files later when we work with our more visually designed SpriteKit game example.

7. Build and run the app to see Apple's default SpriteKit project, which has `Hello World` written in Chalkduster font and a rotating spaceship appears where you click or tap on the screen.

An overview of the SpriteKit structure and objects

Before we add our code, let's use this template to get an idea on how SpriteKit's basic objects, functions, and flow work.

As we stated in the previous chapter, `AppDelegate.swift` is the main entry point. The code then moves to `GameViewController.swift`, which is a child of the `UIViewController` class that imports the SpriteKit framework. The following code is written in the `viewDidLoad()` function of `GameViewController`:

```
override func viewDidLoad() {
    super.viewDidLoad()
    if let scene = GameScene(fileNamed:"GameScene") {
        // Configure the view.
        let skView = self.view as! SKView
        skView.showsFPS = true
        skView.showsNodeCount = true
        /* Sprite Kit applies additional optimizations
           to improve rendering performance */
        skView.ignoresSiblingOrder = true
        /* Set the scale mode to scale to fit the window */
        scene.scaleMode = .AspectFill
        skView.presentScene(scene)
    }
}
```

Using the keyword `override`, this version of `viewDidLoad()` can now either add to or well override the parent class's functionality. `super.viewDidLoad()` calls the parent class's original functionality and then it works its own custom functionality. This is how Swift handles the OOP concept of inheritance.

Next, we see how a game scene is first created with `GameViewController`. A major aspect of SpriteKit is that it works in scenes that are members of the `SKScene` class, which are themselves children of the `SKNode` class. The `SKNode` classes are the main building blocks of nearly every object in SpriteKit. Be it sprites, lights, videos, effects, physics fields, audio files (`SKAudioNodes`), cameras (`SKCameraNodes`), or labels/UI objects, they are `SKNode` classes. These objects all hold important information, most importantly coordinate information of object's node family. For games, this allows the developer to create custom classes, such as `Enemies`, `GameLights`, `Tiles`, and so on, that all have screen and other information on both parent and child nodes. For example, we can hit every enemy on the screen with an attack by the player by calling an inherited function in a parent `Enemy` class. We don't need to check for each individual type of enemy but instead enumerate through the parent nodes in the various game loop functions of `SKScene`:

```
enumerateChildNodesWithName("player", usingBlock: block)
```

Do you remember the block/closure call in PikiPop? To actually use it in the `didSimulatePhysics()` function of `SKScene`, we call the `enumerateChildNodesWithName` function of `SKNode` to target only those nodes in the scene and have that block of code run for each member in the scene with that name.

```
playerNode.name = "player"
```

The name is simply a *string* that can be set using the `SKNode.name` property. Have every custom node initiate with a given name (or change during game play), and you have a whole group of objects you can single out in the scene.

You can find more on `SKNode` in Apple's official documentation at `https://developer.apple.com/library/ios/documentation/SpriteKit/Reference/SKNode_Ref/`.

Scene transitions and the choice of code, storyboards, and/or SKS files

The `GameScene.swift` class in our project inherits from `SKScene`, and it is there that the game loop / rendering functions we mentioned earlier occur. SpriteKit runs on scenes, and scenes can be transitioned and segued to and from it.

In the previous chapter, we showed how to structure a game using storyboards and segues. SKScene makes it where you don't even have to use storyboards but just straight code to transition. We can use storyboards, and we can also visually design each individual scene using .sks files or a combination of all three methods. With code, SKScene can transition with the SKTransition objects and functions. Actually, as we'll see with SwiftSweeper, we can just use code to manually refresh assets in the scene to do *transitions*. This method is rather old fashioned and not as elegant as SKTransition storyboards and SKS files, so let's take a quick look at how to transition scenes in code with SKTransition, storyboards, and briefly into SKS files via code. Later, and in the next chapter, we will focus much more on the visual SKS files since every update to iOS and Xcode continues to put the focus on these visual tools to shorten the coding time and workflow.

An SKTransition example

The following code changes the game's scene:

```
override func touchesBegan(touches:
Set<UITouch>, withEvent event: UIEvent?) {
  super.touchesBegan(touches, withEvent: event)
  if let location = touches.first?.locationInNode(self) {
      let touchedNode = self.nodeAtPoint(location)
      if touchedNode.name == "SceneChangeButton" {
          let transition = SKTransition.revealWithDirection(
          SKTransitionDirection.Up, duration: 1.0)

          let scene = AnotherGameScene(size: self.scene!.size)
          scene.scaleMode = SKSceneScaleMode.AspectFill
          self.scene!.view!.presentScene(scene,
          transition: transition)
      }
  }
}
```

The SKTransition classes are really just types of segues. As in the preceding code, the transition is a directional switch to the next scene with the SKTransitionDirection.Up enumerator type. As we saw in GameViewController, the new scene is created with the similar functions that control the scene's view size and aspect ratio and then presents that scene to the unwrapped view with self. scene!.view!.presentScene(scene, transition: transition).

Also note that this takes place in the same function as we see in our current project's GameScene.swift class, override func touchesBegan(touches: Set<UITouch>, withEvent event: UIEvent?) {}. This is the function that handles touch gestures from the player and checks whether the name of the node touched matches the SceneChangeButton string.

More on SKTransition and other neat transition effects you can give your games can be found here in the official documentation:

https://developer.apple.com/library/prerelease/ios/documentation/ SpriteKit/Reference/SKTransition_Ref/

 As of Swift 2.0 / iOS 9, this touch delegate function takes in a parameter that is a set of UITouches via touches: Set<UITouch> and an optional UIEvent. This is a change from past Swift iterations and could change in future updates.

A SKScene/storyboard example

Here's the code for a SKScene/storyboard example:

```
@IBAction func buttonPressed(button:UIButton)
{
    // Remove button from the view
    button.removeFromSuperview()
    if let scene = GameScene.unarchiveFromFile("GameScene")
    as? GameScene {
        // Configure the view.
        let skView = self.view as SKView
        skView.showsFPS = false
        skView.showsNodeCount = false

        //used for optimization of SKView
        skView.ignoresSiblingOrder = true

        scene.scaleMode = .AspectFill
        skView.presentScene(scene)
    }
}
```

As we saw in the previous chapter, using the visual help of storyboard files can give us great visual road maps to our apps, both game and non-game. The preceding code uses a link to an @IBAction linkage on a storyboard file to set a new scene.

Storyboards in games can be great for the prototyping phase when we know just the general structure of our game, and can be perfect for the game's menu navigations or even for all individual game scenes*.

The button itself is removed before the transition via the button. removeFromSuperview() call to prevent a memory leak caused by the new scene being drawn over what could have been an unseen menu button—unseen to the player but not to the game's memory stack.

*It's usually the best practice to only use storyboards for overall navigation menus and not for each individual level/scene. The SKScene and SKNode functionality can let us reuse similar scene structures and save much of the coding for similarly structured levels. Games with many levels could turn our storyboards into a web of confusing structures and thus undo their initial purpose. Scenes with the actual gameplay could just be in their own single view controller in the storyboard, and we'd have the pause, share, and other menus be controlled by storyboard segues.

SKScene transitions with SKS files

A .sks file is a special SpriteKit scene file that can allow the creation of a scene as well as the placement of the player, particles, enemies, and level assets in a visual, drag and drop way. Transitioning to a visually designed .sks file in Swift is the same as our initial SKTransition example.

```
override func touchesBegan(touches: Set<NSObject>,
withEvent event: UIEvent) {
    /* Called when a touch begins */
    let introNode = childNodeWithName("introNode")

    if (introNode != nil) {
        let fadeAway = SKAction.fadeOutWithDuration(1.0)

        introNode?.runAction(fadeAway, completion: {
            let doors = SKTransition.doorwayWithDuration(1.0)
            let gameScene = GameScene(fileNamed: "GameScene")
            self.view?.presentScene(gameScene, transition: doors)
        })
    }
}
```

The creation of the `gameScene` constant with the `SKScene` initializer `fileNamed` and then presenting that scene to the view works the same with either the `.swift` file or `.sks` file. This gives us the flexibility to both code and/or visually design our game scenes. In the case of `SwiftSweeper`, we will do the more code-centric methodology, but feel free to build on this game on your own if you wish with either more code, Storyboards, and/or with visually designed `SpriteKitScene` (`.sks`) files.

Assets, sprites, and icons

As of Xcode 7, game assets are placed in the `Assets.xcassets` folder. Previous versions of Xcode might have had an `Images.xcassets` folder for the game's icons and sprites, but this has changed and might continue to change with each new iOS release.

An image from Apple's WWDC15 conference

Starting with iOS 9 and Xcode 7, the `assets` folder was given even more flexibility with the ability to handle the various app icon sizes, the launch image, sets of images, and sprite atlases. This also allows us to develop with various memory saving capabilities introduced in iOS 9 like **app slicing / app thinning** and on-demand resources. The app slicing/thinning feature makes sure that only the assets relevant to the device are downloaded, which saves space on the player's iPhone or iPad. On-demand resources let us tag assets that are available in the device's memory only during certain parts of our games. This way, we can create even larger games for our players to experience without taxing the sometimes-limited space in the Apple family of devices.

You can find more on app slicing/thinning at `https://developer.apple.com/library/prerelease/ios/documentation/IDEs/Conceptual/AppDistributionGuide/AppThinning/AppThinning.html`.

When setting up your game for on-demand services, something that could be great to know in the initial planning of your games, can be found in the official documentation at `https://developer.apple.com/library/prerelease/ios/documentation/FileManagement/Conceptual/On_Demand_Resources_Guide/`.

Sprite atlases and animating sprites

SwiftSweeper actually doesn't use animating sprites; as we'll see, it simply uses Unicode emoticon characters to animate the screen. Yet, we can't discuss SpriteKit and 2D game development without mentioning sprites, animating and optimizing them with texture atlases/sprite sheets, could we? A sprite atlas is a collection of images bundled into a single image, also known as a **sprite sheet** or **texture atlas**. While developing 2D games, it is highly recommended to use texture atlases as opposed to various image sets because to the renderer, texture atlases will equate to far fewer draw calls and thus can make sure that your game runs at that needed 60 fps. The `Collectables.atlas` folder in `Assets.xcassets` could hold all of your game's collectables and with the `SKTextureAtlas` class, efficiently draw those collectables to the screen. When storing the images to say the player's idle, walking, and jumping animations, we use texture atlases to store them.

Creating a texture atlas is very simple and is presented as follows:

1. Simply click on your `Assests.xcassets` folder and right-click on an empty part of the folder's hierarchy.

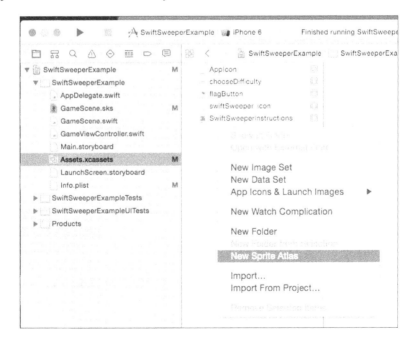

2. Click on **New Sprite Atlas** and just like this, we have a folder where we can store various sprites for our game.

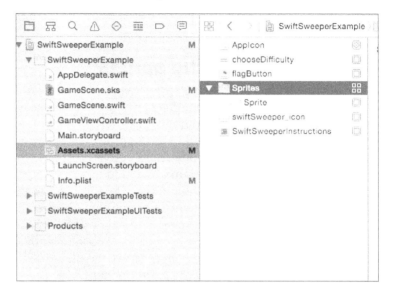

3. Make sure to name the folder based on how you wish to categorize the groups of sprites. You'd need this name when referencing them in code.

To create a reference to this atlas in code and animate the sprites, we use SKTextureAtlas as follows:

```
let PlayerAtlas = SKTextureAtlas(named:"Player.atlas")

let textures = map(1...4) { number in
            PlayerAtlas.textureNamed("player_sprite_normal_
            \(number)")
            }
            let anim = SKAction.animateWithTextures(textures,
            timePerFrame: self.animationRefreshRate_)
            let idleAnimation = SKAction.repeatActionForever(anim)
            self.runAction(idleAnimation)
```

First, this code creates an SKTextureAtlas reference to the player's sprite atlas using the initializer SKTextureAtlas(named:"Player.atlas"). Then, we create an array of textures using one of Swift's orders block map(NSRange) {...}. This is a closure block that iterates through the textures in the sprite atlas based on the range specified in the map call. The number object is a simple index object we can use to represent the index of the mapping.

This is done because our player has these sprite names for the normal/idle animation:

```
"player_sprite_normal_1", "player_sprite_normal_2",
"player_sprite_normal_3", "player_sprite_normal_4"
```

Since we know that the sprite animations are named with an indexed naming structure, it's better to use Swift's functional programming tools, such as `map()`, here to simplify the code. 2D Sprites with many frame-by-frame animations (games such as Metal Slug) could be iterated through in such a fashion.

`SKTextureAtlas` also has a class function named `preloadTextureAtlases` we can use to preload an array of texture atlases:

```
SKTextureAtlas.preloadTextureAtlases([PIKIATLAS,BGATLAS,
COLLECTABLESATLAS,HUDATLAS, OBSTACLESATLAS])
{
  //perform other tasks while loading TextureAtlases
}
```

This is great to make sure that a stage's sprites are loaded before entering the stage.

Creating our game logic

For the sake of simplicity, MineSweeper won't have many different assets or any sprite textures. It instead uses Swift's Unicode emoticon character capabilities and `UIView` calls to design the game's graphics in a rather old-fashioned, very MineSweeper-like way.

Not only do we do this to give us a somewhat simplistic starting point, but to show how Swift code and SpriteKit classes can let us create the entire game's logic and flow without the initial need of sprite assets. This way, if developing as a team or by yourself, the game can be made before doing the sometimes grueling process of making wonderful visual assets. Thinking with code and structure first can ensure that you have a working prototype that you can polish later with sprites, music, and atmosphere.

We've so far left SwiftSweeper waiting as just a shell of the SpriteKit game template. It's about time we get to the game's model:

1. First, let's add our image assets. For more information, visit `https://mega.co.nz/#!XhEgCRgJ!4QqKMl1l1P4opWU7OH2wEN_noVQ86z5mxEyLuyUrcQo`.

    This is a link to the `Assets.xcassets` folder of `SwiftSweeper`. We can add these individually, but the simplest way is to just replace your project's `Assets.xcassets` folder directly in your computer where your project's folder is located. You can have Xcode open while you do this, it'll automatically update from the original template files.

2. Next, let's add the sound files from the following URL:

    `https://mega.co.nz/#!T5dUnJZb!NUT837QQnKeQbTpI8Jd8ISJMx7TnXvucZSY7Frw5gcY`

3. Add the sounds by doing the following:

    1. Right-click on the `SwiftSweeperExample` folder that holds the Swift files and then go to **New** | **Group** from the menu.

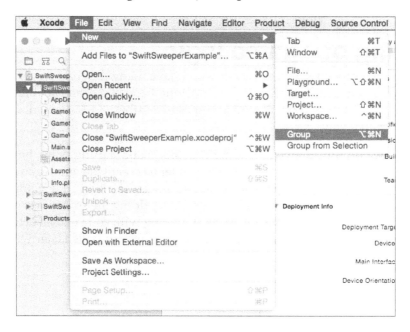

2. Name this folder `Sounds` and drag it to the bottom of the files within the same `SwiftSweeperExample` folder.

3. Right-click the `Sounds` folder and select `Add Files To "SwiftSweeperExample"`.

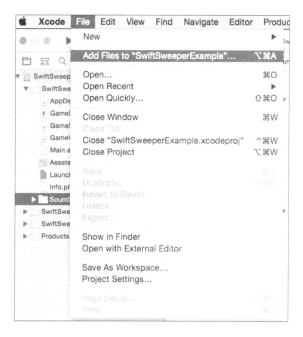

4. Add the sounds from the `SwiftSweeperSounds` folder, and they should now be in your project.

All of the assets should be now in the project, so now we can build our game. Let's first start with the actual tiles.

Now create a new Swift file, name it `Tile`, and paste the following code into the file:

```
class Tile{
    //Properties
//(1)
    let row : Int
    let column : Int
//(2)
    var isTileDown = false
    var isFlagged = false
    var isAMine = false
```

```
// (3)
    //Mines counter
    var nearbyMines:Int = 0
// (4)
    init(row:Int, col: Int){
        self.row = row
        self.column = col
    }
}
```

Here are some stepwise logic we adhere to while creating tiles:

1. While building any code logic, we usually place the properties about this object at the top. We know that each tile in a game of MineSweeper will be part of a row and a column. The number of the row and the column this tile will have during gameplay won't change during the course of a single round, so we make them constants with the keyword `let` and set them with the type `Int` as we know that you can't have fractions of a row or a column, at least in terms of the tile objects.

2. A tile can have a few different states. It could be already tapped, it could have a flag placed on it, and if it's a a mine. Since these are true/false properties, we set them with as Boolean variables `isTileDown`, `isFlagged`, and `isAMine`. We set them to `false` initially.

3. Tiles in MineSweeper count how many tiles around them are mines, so we create the integer counter `nearbyMines` to hold that information.

4. When an instance of a tile object is created, we want the game to set its row and column number placement on the `GameBoard`, so we create the default initializer, `init`, to have two parameter inputs for both the row and column.

That's all we need for the `Tile` objects, so let's move on to setting the button functionality of these `Tile` objects with the `MineTileButton` class.

Create a new Swift file and name it `MineTileButton` and paste the following code into it:

```
// (1)
import UIKit
class MineTileButton : UIButton {
// (2)
    var tile:Tile
    let tileSize:CGFloat
```

```
//(3)
    init(tileButton:Tile, size:CGFloat) {
        self.tile = tileButton
        self.tileSize = size

        let x = CGFloat(self.tile.column) * tileSize
        let y = CGFloat(self.tile.row) * tileSize
        let tileBoundingFrame = CGRectMake(x, y,
        tileSize, tileSize)
        super.init(frame: tileBoundingFrame)

    }
//(4)
    required init(coder aDecoder: NSCoder) {
        fatalError("init(coder:) has not been implemented")
    }
//(5)
    //button text;
    //replace button with an SKSprite for better GUI interface?
    func getTileLabelText() -> String {
        if !self.tile.isAMine {
            if self.tile.nearbyMines == 0 {
                return "0"
            }else {
                return "\(self.tile.nearbyMines)"
            }
        }
//(6)
        return "⊠"
    }
}
```

Here's the explanation of the code:

1. Since we are creating a `UIButton` object, we import the UIKit framework for this object.

2. These are the properties of this button object. We need a `Tile` object named `tile` to reference, a `CGFloat` size named `tileSize` to represent the rectangle this button will occupy.

3. The initializer for this class takes in a `Tile` object named `tileButton` and a `CGFloat` named `size`. We assign the class's own tile to `tileButton` and `tileSize` to `size` and then we make a square named `tileBoundingFrame` with the `CGRectMake()` method. This is done just after we set an *x* and *y* value of `CGFloat` to the square based on the `tileSize`. The `UIButton` parent `init(frame: )` initializer uses the `tileBoundingFrame` as the parameter via `super.init(frame: tileBoundingFrame)`.

4. Since Xcode 5, the `init` function is needed mainly to keep the compiler happy while dealing with UI objects.

5. The function `getTileLabelText()` returns a string based on the status of the `tile` object. If the tile is not a mine, we know that we have to either place something for there being no tiles; traditionally, this is just a blank space or an empty `""` string, but for now, we are just placing 0 there, leaving the logic open for customization. Honestly, we could simply return the nested if-else statement's return `\(self.tile.nearbyMines)`, and it'd return the same result. As we see, it's returning the particular `Tile` object's `nearbyMines` property.

6. If the tile is a mine, then we return the collision Unicode emoji character. The `getTileLabelText()` function is called when the player taps an `unflagged` tile.

7. Swift's ability to use Unicode character symbols can be a great visual aid in the planning process of your games. The collision Unicode emoji used in line (6) is `U+1F4A5 (128165)`. If you see only a square box and not the red explosion-like character, it can be seen in the full project download mentioned earlier in the chapter or at the following link.

 Find more information on this emoji at `http://www.charbase.com/1f4a5-unicode-collision-symbol`.

GameBoard

Now that we have our tile object and button logic that will represent each tile object named `MineTileButton`, we need to create an object representing the collection of these objects, that is, `GameBoard`.

The full `GameBoard.swift` code is a bit too large to show here in its entirety, so we will summarize its main features and segments.

We can view the entire code either in the full project link mentioned earlier in the chapter, or directly below in order to copy to your current game project file:

https://mega.co.nz/#!X8FB2aAK

For our `GameBoard`, we are looking to create a tiled board of 10x10 size that also has three levels of difficulty: easy, medium, and hard. To create the difficulty, we simply use an enumerator named `difficulty` to store the game's difficulty levels.

The most important properties of `GameBoard` include `boardSize_` (which is set to `10` in this case), a variable that will represent the number of mines that will be placed named `mineRandomizer`, the number of mines active on the board named `mineCount`, and the Tile objects that will populate the board named `tiles`.

Make a note of the syntax used for the `tiles` property:

```
var tiles:[[Tile]] = []
```

In this way, we can create an ordered 2D array (or matrix) in Swift*. The `GameBoard` object will basically store an array of an array of `Tile` type objects.

*Swift does have more ways to express matrices, for example, we can use Structs to define our own unique matrices. As at the time of this publication, Swift does not have its own true functionality for fixed length arrays, as we see in various C languages. However, using the nested braces `[[]]` is fine for what we are trying to accomplish.

The initializer for `GameBoard`, `init(selectedDifficulty:difficulty){}`, takes in the player-selected difficulty as it's single parameter then builds the board based on the `boardSize` property and then uses the following nested for-in loop to populate the entire board with `Tile` objects:

```
for row in 0 ..< boardSize_ {
    var tilesRow:[Tile] = []
    for col in 0 ..< boardSize_ {
        let tile = Tile(row: row, col: col)
        tilesRow.append(tile)
    }
    tiles.append(tilesRow)
}
```

Since the `tiles` object is a 2D array, we first need to perform this nested loop that first creates a 1D array of `Tile` objects (named `tilesRow`) for each row and then add a tile for each column in that row with the `.append` function. The main tiles 2D array is then appended that `tilesRow` array.

If you wish to make a `GameBoard` instance that is a rectangle or of another shape, you'd have to take into account the differing column and row amounts. This would make the nested for-loop have more complexity by needing a separate `columnSize` and `rowSize` property. Many puzzle games will make their boards look complex to the player but might still keep their internal structures simple to either squares or rectangles by instead filling in that tile with a nonplayable section or background/transparent tile.

It's a way for a developer to cut corners while at the same time allowing complex functionality and design. It's why we built this game with separate classes representing the Tiles, the tile button functionalities, and the game board layout.

Using inheritance, we can continue to customize what each tile does and thus allow a myriad of features based on a simple foundation.

It's why video games have always been the poster children to make the most out of object-oriented design.

Don't worry if at first it's tough to get a full understanding of this, as nested loops tend to be brain twisters. Just observe how the interior for-loop won't exit until it's done filling in columns based on the `boardSize_` property. This kind of loop is made easier with the fact that the rows and columns are all equal at 10.

The initializer then calls the `resetBoard()` function, which resets the `mineCount` to 0, and does two more nested for-loops:

```
for row in 0 ..< boardSize_ {
        for column in 0 ..< boardSize_ {
            self.createRandomMineTiles(tiles[row][column])
            tiles[row][column].isTileDown = false
        }
    }
```

This board-iterating for-loop randomly sets which tiles are mines using the `createRandomMineTiles()` function as well as resets the tiles to being untouched with the `tiles[row][column].isTileDown = false` call. The `createRandomMineTiles()` function works off the current difficulty level, particularly the `mineRandomizer` property that is determined in the `implementDifficulty()` function. The higher the `mineRandomizer` value, the less of a chance the iterated tile will be made into a mine.

The next nested for-loop in `resetBoard()` is the following:

```
for row in 0 ..< boardSize_ {
        for column in 0 ..< boardSize_ {
            self.calculateNearbyMines(tiles[row][column])
        }
    }
```

This iterates through every tile on the board and sets the number the player will see if tapped. That number of course being the number of mines surrounding a non-mine tile, that is, the `nearbyMines` property of the `Tile` class.

This rather complex chain of calculations begins with the `calculateNearbyMines()` function and runs through the array/tile index calculating functions, `getNearbyTiles()` and `getAdjacentTileLocation()`. We provided various detailed comments in each of these functions to get a better understanding on how they work. It's advised that you read the intricate details on how it's done but to not muddy an already complex game logic explanation, take notes on the following line in `getNearbyTiles()`:

```
let nearbyTileOffsets =
    [(-1,-1), //bottom left corner from selected tile
            (0,-1),  //directly below
            (1,-1),  //bottom right corner
            (-1,0),  //directly left
            (1,0),   //directly right
            (-1,1),  //top left corner
            (0,1),   //directly above
            (1,1)]   //top right corner
```

If any line in these three complex functions is to be understood, it's this one. The `nearbyTileOffset` object is an explicitly written array of tuples, which contains every offset that could exist around a single 2D tile. Actually, it's best to think of each member of this array as an (x,y) 2D Vector.

Thus, as commented in the preceding code, the offset of (-1,-1) would be to the bottom left of the tile since x = -1 (left 1) and y = -1 (down 1). Similarly, (1,0) is to the right, (1,1) is the top-right corner.

We also have to take into account that some tiles are on the edge and/or column of the board, thus some of the tile offsets won't return the reference to another tile; they'll instead return nil.

```
for (rowOffset,columnOffset) in nearbyTileOffsets {

  //optional since tiles in the corners/edges could have less
  than 8 surrounding tiles and thus could have a nil value
            let ajacentTile:Tile? = getAjacentTileLocation(
            selectedTile.row+rowOffset, col:
            selectedTile.column+columnOffset)
            //if validAjacentTile isn't nil, add the
Tile object to the nearby Tile array
            if let validAjacentTile = ajacentTile {
                nearbyTiles.append(validAjacentTile)
            }
        }
}
```

This for-loop in getNearbyTiles() not only checks the offsets of every tile, but also, using the call to getAjacentTileLocation(), accounts for edge or corner tiles.

Again, these three functions are rather complex, even in a less line-by-line / semi-generic explanation of their functionality. So, don't worry if you don't understand the flow/order at first.

Finally, for resetBoard(), we can't win the game without knowing if the player got every non-mine tile, so we get that information with the line:

```
numOfTappedTilesToWin_ = totalTiles_ - mineCount
```

When the player's number of completed moves (counted in the GameScene class) equals numOfTappedTilesToWin, the player wins!

This is all done before the player makes the first move! This is done in order to have the values already predetermined. Yes, we could make some of these calculations during the player's touch, but dealing with boilerplate game logic is usually fast enough to prepare the game at load time so that we can use the game play to focus on effects, sequences, and other visual notifications during the game loop.

This functionality is controlled by the GameScene.swift file, which we will summarize next.

Putting it all together in GameScene.swift

We now have the core of SwiftSweeper's logic set up, but now it's time to present it in our `SKScene` provided by the game template, `GameScene`. This scene uses the game/rendering loop functions that we mentioned at the beginning of the chapter.

The SwiftSweeper version of `GameScene.swift` is rather large at about 800 lines of code, so like `GameBoard`, we won't be going over it line by line but instead we'll be summarizing some of the important aspects of the scene. As stated previously, every update to Xcode and iOS brings more visual ways of setting up these scenes, so getting to know every line of code in this example isn't necessary, but still recommended if you really wish to dive deep into how to use code to present SpriteKit game scenes.

The full code can be found in the full project link mentioned earlier in the chapter or (if you've been building it from scratch throughout the chapter) at the link mentioned here:

```
https://mega.co.nz/#!PgljBL7b
```

We used various `//MARK:` comments to section off parts of this code, so you can navigate easier. After copying the code into your project, you could build and run the app. As long as everything was placed into the project correctly, you should have a working version of SwiftSweeper running on your phone or in the phone simulators. Play through it a bit to get an idea what is being done in GameScene to present the game. Sometimes, seeing a game in action lets us see the code behind it better. If any errors pop up, something went wrong and if all else fails, you can download the completed project from `https://github.com/princetrunks/ SwiftSweeper`.

The first visual entry point in GameScene, `didMoveToView()`, is actually rather small as follows:

```
override func didMoveToView(view: SKView){
        self.backgroundColor = UIColor.whiteColor()
        stageView_ = view
        loadInstructions()
    }
```

We simply set the background color to white and load the instructions. Again, we didn't say that this was meant to be a beautiful-looking game.

The `loadInstructions()` function manually places the instructions sprite on the screen and sets the `currentGameState_` enum to `.Instructions`. A **game state** or **state machine** is common game development methodology that instructs characters, the player, and the game itself what state it is in. This could be used to make sure that certain parts of the gameplay don't happen in parts they aren't suppose to. iOS 9 / Xcode 7 introduced the framework; we'll dive into more later chapters named GamePlayKit, which, among other game logic functions, works with state machines that can be modular and independent from a specific scene. Components from the class `SKComponents` and more modern usage of `SKAction`, also introduced in iOS 9, work in the same way, independent from OOP inheritance. Think of more dynamic/usable versions of protocols.

The next overall step in the GameScene is the `chooseDifficultyMenu()` that came with the `removeInstructions()` function, which was called after the player taps the screen. This tap is checked in the function we mentioned in a few examples prior, `touchesBegan()`, using the game state as a logic check:

```
override func touchesBegan(touches: Set<UITouch>,
withEvent event: UIEvent?) {
    /* Called when a touch begins */
     for touch in touches {
        //flag button Pressed
        if CGRectContainsPoint(flagButton_.frame,
        touch.locationInNode(self)) {
            flagButtonPressed()
        }
        //instructions removed when tapped
        if CGRectContainsPoint(instructionsSprite_.frame,
        touch.locationInNode(self)) && currentGameState_
        == .Instructions {
            removeInstructions()
        }
     }
  }
```

Note how the `touchesBegan` function is actually rather simple. It only checks if we tapped the flag button or if we tapped on the instructions. What about the tiles? Well, remember that we made these tiles all members of `UIButton` with the `MineTileButton` class. Here's the function that controls this:

```
func tileButtonTapped(sender: MineTileButton) {
    //exit function if not playing the game
    if (currentGameState_ != .MineTap && currentGameState_
    != .FlagPlanting){
```

```
            return
        }
        //reveals the underlying tile, only if the game is
        in the main state, aka MineTap
        if (!sender.tile.isTileDown && currentGameState_
        == .MineTap) {
            sender.tile.isTileDown = true
            sender.setTitle("\(sender.getTileLabelText())",
            forState: .Normal)
            //sender.backgroundColor = UIColor.lightGrayColor()
            //mine HIT!
            if sender.tile.isAMine {
                //sender.backgroundColor = UIColor.orangeColor()
                self.mineHit()
            }
            //counts the moves; also used in calculating a win
            moves_++
        }
        else if (!sender.tile.isTileDown && currentGameState_
        == .FlagPlanting){
            self.flagPlant(sender)
        }
    }
}
```

Members of the UIButton class send out a reference of what has been tapped to the scene. In this game, is an object of the type, MineTileButton. Using the game state to check if it's logical to the scene, we either end the round if a mine is hit with the mineHit() function or we increment the moves performed (used to calculate the win by comparing it to numOfTappedTilesToWin_ calculated at the start of the round). If the game state is .FlagPlanting, then we instead deal with the logic behind planting a flag on the tiles. Tiles with flags don't react to .MineTap game state taps and thus, if you put a flag on the wrong tile, you won't get the win until you uncover all of the non-mine tiles.

Through the rest of the code, we'll find a timer, alerts for the player based on the outcome, and even the ability to save times per difficulty levels using the class functions of the NSUserDefaults class.

Again, it's not exactly all that visually elegant, but intricate in code and most importantly a fully functioning game. We advise you to check out more of the code in GameScene.swift, but one major issue to our design one might have caused in the beginning is that this only works with iPhones.

Using visual tools such as autolayout, seen briefly in the previous chapter, will allow easier design changes for the entire family of iOS devices. Since many of the visual assets in SwiftSweeper's GameScene were manually placed in the view (particularly the instructions), we'd have to account for every device type in code. This is possible, but as the family of devices grows, manual code used for screen visuals could be broken rather easily in future iOS updates and device announcements. That's why in our next chapter about SceneKit and later, we will mostly diverge from this code-centric structure and embrace the hands-on tools and newer frameworks such as GamePlaykit from Xcode 7 and later.

DemoBots

As at the initial publication of this book, *WWDC15* recently completed and gave us a great new SpriteKit demo project for iOS 9 and Xcode 7 named **DemoBots**.

DemoBots is a SpriteKit project provided by Apple that uses components, state machines, on-demand services, GameplayKit, ReplayKit, and more!

The full project documentation to DemoBots can be found at `https://developer.apple.com/library/prerelease/ios/samplecode/DemoBots/Introduction/Intro.html`.

To see it in action from *WWDC15*, see the video and PDF file from the *Deeper into GameplayKit with DemoBots* keynote:

`https://developer.apple.com/videos/wwdc/2015/?id=609`

The SpriteKit keynote can be found here:

`https://developer.apple.com/videos/wwdc/2015/?id=604`

DemoBots's gameplay even has easily editable enemy AI / navigation schemes uses the `SKCameraNode` introduced in iOS 9 that follows the player and doesn't move the scene around in the view as in past versions of SpriteKit. As we mentioned at the beginning of the chapter, mimicking the tools we see in multiplatform game engines.

Summary

We went through a number of topics here in this chapter. We first spoke on why SpriteKit was a welcomed addition to iOS after years of developers only having third-party gaming frameworks, such as Cocos2D and Sparrow. We discussed how SpriteKit fits in the game development ecosystem as rather powerful, multiplatform game engines, such as Unity and Unreal Engine, continue to become more prominent. Next, we went into the SpriteKit game loop and rendering cycle that is used by `SKScene`. Then, we began to build our demo tile game, `SwiftSweeper`, and dove more into the basic structure of SpriteKit's most prominent object classes. The iOS 9 `assets` folder was reviewed in addition to texture atlases and how to animate sprites using these asset tools. Then, we went into the rather complex logic and code that goes into mimicking a tile game such as MineSweeper.

Next, we move on to iOS's 3D game development framework, SceneKit, where we will diverge more towards the visual tools Apple now brings to us since iOS 8 / iOS 9. We'll take less of a code-centric methodology now that we know the basic scene/code structure that both SceneKit and SpriteKit share. SpriteKit scenes can overlay SceneKit scenes, so we will see some of what we hinted at with Apple's own DemoBots demo shortly.

4
SceneKit and 3D Game Design

For this chapter, we will be going over the iOS framework used for 3D game development known as SceneKit. SceneKit first became available in iOS 7 but originally was just used for MacOS development. Previously, developers had to code 3D games using OpenGL or third-party frameworks and engines, such as Cocos3D, Unreal Engine, Havok, and Unity. As the graphical power in the iOS family of devices improved, so did the need for an immersive, hands-on first-party 3D game design engine. SceneKit shortly became available for iOS giving developers an Xcode built-in solution to make 3D games.

In the previous chapter, we approached iOS game development in a more code-based methodology. We'll still be working in some code, but since the introduction of Xcode 5 and Xcode 6, Apple has provided some great demos that show how the IDE can be just as visually dynamic of a game engine as multiplatform game engines are. The benefit of using Xcode and the SpriteKit/SceneKit frameworks over those engines is that you have a dedicated design environment for a specific platform. In our case, that platform is iOS and the Apple family of devices. As iOS frequently updates and continues to give new features, Xcode and these frameworks will update with it. Updates to the multiplatform engines usually occur at a later date with sometimes the additional need to install plugins to ensure that your app runs smoothly in future updates.

In addition to the very dynamic and tool-rich DemoBots SpriteKit demo, the *June 2015 World Wide Developer's Conference* also introduced a wonderful SceneKit demo named Fox. The Fox demo also makes use of features introduced in iOS 9 that we can use for either SpriteKit or SceneKit, such as reusable actions, components, and state machines.

In this chapter, we will go over the basics of SceneKit and we will make a simple SceneKit scene (known as SCNScene) using both code and the visual design tools Xcode provides. We will then add physics, lights, and particles to our SceneKit objects and scene. We will then wrap up with a look into the *WWDC15* Fox Demo and some of the features/APIs it uses, which became available in iOS 8 and iOS 9.

In the previous chapter, we left out much of these asset creation features in our discussion on SpriteKit. With SpriteKit scene files, (.sks), we can also create game assets, such as lights, physics fields, bounding boxes/physics constraints, normal maps, textures, entire levels, and characters in the same fashion that SceneKit scene files (.scn) work. We will at times show the SpriteKit method to similar features.

Since SpriteKit and SceneKit scene assets work similarly and can be together in the same scene (thanks to their inherit node/tree functionality), we thought that it was best to save the visual and asset tool discussion for this chapter. The previous chapter's talk on the game/render loop and much of the scene code functionality will work in SceneKit much like it did previously in SpriteKit.

So in other words, we are already set up to dive right into SceneKit.

SceneKit basics and working with nodes

Like SpriteKit, SceneKit is based on the concept of nodes. SpriteKit objects are children of the SKNode class, while SceneKit objects are children of the SCNNode class.

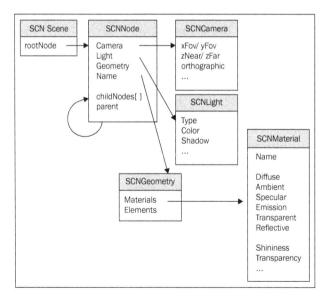

The preceding image is the SceneGraph hierarchy from Apple's SceneKit introduction. As we see, SceneKit has various nodes that branch off from the `SCNScene` class. These include the generic `SCNNode` for lights, geometry, and the camera.

Nodes are a tree data structure that can have other nodes added to them and have information of other nodes in the structure. As seen in the preceding graph, it's shown with the `childNode[]` array and parent properties. Spatial information, such as position, scale, and orientation, can be received from these properties. This is what makes nodes unique to other parent-child structuring in object-oriented design (OOD).

In SpriteKit, we'd typically add a node to our scene or to another node within our scene via the `addChild()` function. In SceneKit, the same functionality is done with `addChildNode()`. For example, the main root node in a SceneKit scene is the `SCNScene` node that is placed in the `SCNView` node, that is, the framework's unique version of the `UIView` class. To add a basic sphere object to our scene, we'd do the following:

```
let sphereGeometry = SCNSphere(radius: 1.0)
let sphereNode = SCNNode(geometry: sphereGeometry)
self.rootNode.addChildNode(sphereNode)
```

As stated with SpriteKit, working with nodes in SpriteKit can allow us to group various members of our game scene together into their own parent nodes and make actions on them in one call also iterating through for loops or other iteration calls.

SpriteKit / SceneKit interactivity

One great feature of SceneKit is that we can have a SpriteKit scene overlay our 3D game.

```
self.overlaySKScene = skScene
```

Using the `SCNView` property `overlaySKcene`, we can take an already established `SKScene` node (which can be a character, an animation sequence, an HUD, and more) and have them in our 3D scene.

Want to have a cute sprite animation overlay your 3D character's stage win or maybe want to make a 2.5D game with 2D sprites and physics overlaying a 3D background? Then this is how you can do it.

The most common functionality of mixing SpriteKit with SceneKit is that SpriteKit is the HUD for the SceneKit scene. The lives, collectables, and character icon seen in the earlier Fox demo shows a SpriteKit node overlaying a SceneKit scene.

Nodes in general can help add a functional structure to your game and game scenes. A high reliance on nodes and inheritance in game design doesn't come without its flaws though.

The issue with inheritance-based structuring and game design

Before going forward, we should mention about a certain pitfall that could plague a game that relies too much on the concept of nodes and even the general concept of inheritance-based structuring in OOD. When possible, it's best not to rely too much on inheritance for your game logic and work more with what's known as composite-based structuring. We'll go deeper into this in our next chapter when we talk about the helper game development framework first introduced in iOS 9, GamePlayKit, but here's a glance so that we know that working with inheritance and even nodes might not always be the best solution in our games.

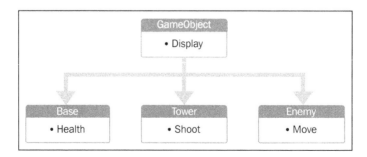

At first glance, one might think that inheritance-based structuring is perfectly made for game development. Many of us familiar with OOD know that we can have generic parent classes or nodes of our game objects, such as an all-encompassing GameObject class, and then use inheritance and polymorphism to work with unique child classes from this base class. For small, simplistic games that will hold true, but games tend to have objects that could share some of the same functionality, but make no sense to have in a parent-child structure.

Take this typical structuring in a tower-based strategy game:

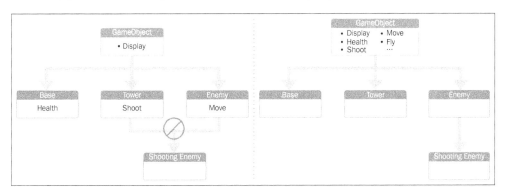

In a typical tower game, we'd have our base, tower, and enemy objects that can all inherit from a generic GameObject class we define. Towers can fire at enemies but so can enemies back at the towers and other player-based objects. Part of good programming and design is to have reusable code and methods. Normally, we'd do this with inheritance. The preceding graph shows two-way inheritance that can solve this. We would then want a ShootingEnemy class that inherits the movement and shooting functionality. We can't do this, as that would involve inheriting from two separate and rather unrelated classes of objects. In OOD, there's only one child-parent relationship. The next solution shown on the right would be to have the generic GameObject class have this functionality. The issue that arises is that our once simple GameObject parent class becomes all but simple and we inevitably want to add additional features and functionalities to objects in our game. In the past, this would involve refactoring tons of code to accommodate what essentially are simple design add-ons. Protocols used to be somewhat of a solution to this as they'd force us to make a class in a certain way, but even they could get confusing and don't involve the implementation of these features.

The solution would be to work with entities and components.

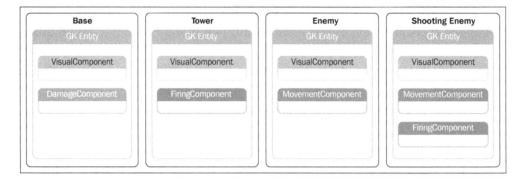

This preceding diagram gives an example of composite-based structuring. With this methodology, we can have components that share similar functionality, being used by multiple and usually unrelated game objects. This way, the generic GameObject class in this example doesn't have to have every possible function of its child class and we can keep Enemy classes as being members of Enemy. The shared functionality can be written once and then used throughout the game and even in the other games we wish to make. iOS 9's SpriteKit demo, DemoBots, and the SceneKit demo mentioned earlier, Fox, both use composite-based structuring for actions and animations.

It's important when thinking with nodes in both SpriteKit and SceneKit that they are used in the context of the View of the MVC model, or in both frameworks, the context of their scenes.

As for scenes in SceneKit, let's move on to making a very basic one.

Our first SceneKit scene – the Xcode template

3D art and animation is a very in-depth topic. We could go on *ad nauseam* about materials, shaders, lighting, sculpting, PVR textures, and all of the topics of what makes great 3D objects for games, movies, architecture, or any other 3D object-based application.

Some of the details of these topics are beyond the scope of this book, so for now, let's keep things simple.

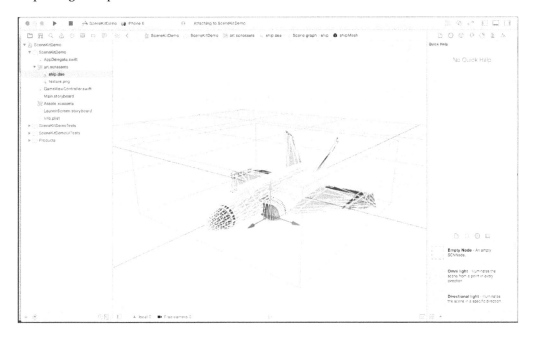

Let's work with the default SceneKit scene and objects that Xcode gives us as a start, as shown in the preceding image:

 As of the time of writing this book, we used the SceneKit template for Xcode 7 – Beta. Based on the version you use, there might be some differences.

1. First, open Xcode, create a new project, and select the **Game** template.

2. Next, name your project, make sure that the **Game Technology** field says **SceneKit**, and click on **Next**.

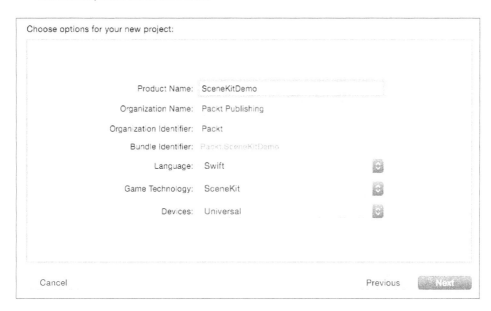

3. The project files and structure are about the same as we saw with SpriteKit but with a couple of differences, particularly the art.scnassets folder. The only difference is that there is now an art.scnassets folder in addition to Assests.xcassets. This is where our 3D objects are held. Click on that folder to see the ship.dae asset that Apple provides.

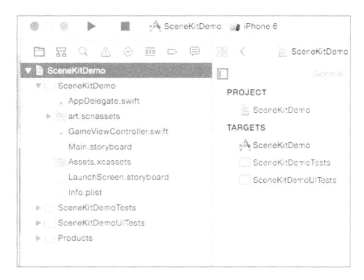

With the SceneKit editor, we can view and edit the following 3D file types:

- DAE
- OBJ
- Alembic
- STL
- PLY

The example given to us is a spaceship of the type DAE and with the `ship.dae` file as the ship's texture file (`texture.png`). Before we look into the code and how the scene works, build and run the program on either your own device or the Xcode device simulator.

From the sample scene, we see our spaceship rotating in front of a black background and we can change its orientation when we swipe the ship. Tapping on the ship causes it to glow red for a moment.

Let's now see what's going on with the code and then we'll get into the tools the editor gives us to edit our objects and scenes without any code.

SceneKit project flow and structure

Like SpriteKit, a SceneKit scene uses the same game-rendering loop as we saw from the previous chapter and the same type of entry point structuring we mentioned in *Chapter 2, Structuring and Planning a Game Using iOS 9 Storyboards and Segues*. We have the `AppDelegate.swift` file that is our entry point with the ability to control special app functionality based on upper level device events, such as the app closing, going into the background, and coming back from being in the background. We also have the launch screen and `Main.storyboard` files as seen before in SpriteKit.

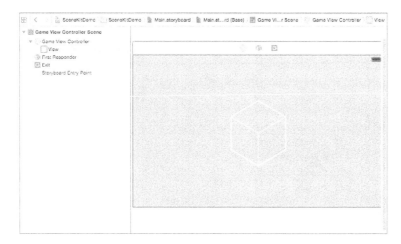

The difference with the `Main.storyboard` file is that it has a SceneKit scene icon, shown with the cube, as seen in the preceding screenshot.

The `ViewController` class the AppDelegate moves to is the `GameViewController. swift` class. This is where all of our code for the demo takes place:

```
override func viewDidLoad() {
        super.viewDidLoad()

        // create a new scene
        let scene = SCNScene(named: "art.scnassets/ship.dae")!
...
```

We see that we begin with the overwritten `viewDidLoad()` function. SceneKit lets us create an entire scene with even an instance of our 3D object/assets, as seen from the unwrapped `let scene = SCNScene(named: "art.scnassets/ship.dae")!` call. This simply creates the scene object. To get the object seen on the screen, we still need to attach this to the `SCNView` node, as we will see later in the function.

Let's look at some more of the code here:

```
//(1) create and add a camera to the scene
   let cameraNode = SCNNode()
   cameraNode.camera = SCNCamera()
   scene.rootNode.addChildNode(cameraNode)
// place the camera
   cameraNode.position = SCNVector3(x: 0, y: 0, z: 15)
//(2) create and add a light to the scene
   let lightNode = SCNNode()
   lightNode.light = SCNLight()
   lightNode.light!.type = SCNLightTypeOmni
   lightNode.position = SCNVector3(x: 0, y: 10, z: 10)
   scene.rootNode.addChildNode(lightNode)
 // create and add an ambient light to the scene
   let ambientLightNode = SCNNode()
   ambientLightNode.light = SCNLight()
   ambientLightNode.light!.type = SCNLightTypeAmbient
   ambientLightNode.light!.color = UIColor.darkGrayColor()
   scene.rootNode.addChildNode(ambientLightNode)
//(3) retrieve the ship node
   let ship = scene.rootNode.childNodeWithName("ship",
   recursively: true)!
//(4) animate the 3d object
        ship.runAction(SCNAction.repeatActionForever(
        SCNAction.rotateByX(0, y: 2, z: 0, duration: 1)))
//(5) retrieve the SCNView
   let scnView = self.view as! SCNView
//set the scene to the view
```

```
    scnView.scene = scene
//(6)allows the user to manipulate the camera
    scnView.allowsCameraControl = true
// show statistics such as fps and timing information
    scnView.showsStatistics = true
// configure the view
    scnView.backgroundColor = UIColor.blackColor()
//(7) add a tap gesture recognizer
    let tapGesture = UITapGestureRecognizer(target: self,
    action: "handleTap:")
        scnView.addGestureRecognizer(tapGesture)
```

The `viewDidLoad()` function mentioned earlier is provided to us in the template. It's actually rather simple to follow and other than the `handleTap()` function, does practically all that's needed to create this scene. Anyone who's created 3D graphics in OpenGL either for iOS or other platforms would appreciate how SceneKit gives us a number of simple upper level controls for the scene and objects. Here are more details of the provided code:

On line `(1)`, an `SCNNode` named cameraNode is created, and we assign the `camera` attribute of `SCNNode` to the `SCNCameraNode` type. Then, the camera is placed in a three-dimensional space using the `SCNVector3()` function on the camera's `position` property. In this case, the camera is placed at ($x:$ 0, $y:$ 0, $z:$ 15). In other words, the x and y coordinates are set at the origin while the camera is moved slightly backwards in the z axis.

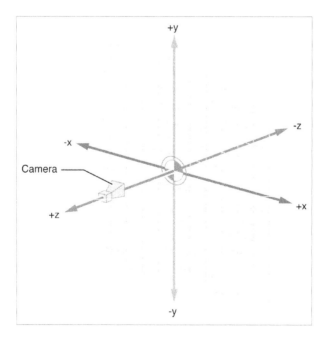

You can find the SceneKit coordinate diagram at `https://developer.apple.com/library/ios/documentation/SceneKit/Reference/SceneKit_Framework/`.

The coordinate system in SceneKit is what's known as a **Right-Handed Coordinate System**. One trick to understand the 3D coordinates is if we take our right hand, make a gun-like gesture out with our thumb up in the air and pointer finger straight ahead of us while our middle finger to the side at a right angle from the pointer finger, we'd have our *x*, *y*, and *z* coordinates. Your middle finger would be on the *x* axis (left/right), your thumb would be on the *y* axis (up/down), and your pointer finger would be on the *z* axis (backward/forward).

In the (2) block of code, we are adding lights to our screen. SceneKit, as well as SpriteKit, lets us create a number of different lighting effects, from ambient occlusion, the use of normal maps, and more. Here, an instance of `SCNNode` is created with the name `lightNode`, and the `SCNNode` property light is assigned the `SCNLight` class type. The first light created and added to the scene is what's known as an `SCNLightTypeOmni` type light, as seen from the implicitly unwrapped call `lightNode.light!.type = SCNLightTypeOmni`. This type of light is typically used more for debugging as the next light added, `ambientLightNode`, would be one of the types used to create the atmosphere to your game. As we see with the line, `ambientLightNode.light!.color = UIColor.darkGrayColor()`, we can assign a color to that light in code.

More information on `SCNLights` can be found at `https://developer.apple.com/library/prerelease/ios/documentation/SceneKit/Reference/SCNLight_Class/index.html`.

We'll soon see how to visually add lights and other aspects of the demo `viewDidLoad()` function to our scene, but it's usually beneficial to understand the boilerplate code behind the scenes.

In the line (3), `let ship = scene.rootNode.childNodeWithName("ship", recursively: true)!` is how we add our `ship` object to the scene's root node. This is not too much different than other objects in the scene. It takes the string `ship` from the name of our `ship.dae` object in the `art.scnassets` folder. The `recursively: true` parameter in the `childNodeWithName` function tells the scene that it should add all child nodes of the object to the scene. Depending on how the 3D object was modeled and rigged in its original 3D model program, the object might have a complex array of child nodes. Setting recursively to `true` will iterate through not just the child nodes but their child nodes as well.

The following long line (part of line (4)) is a compact way of telling the ship to rotate continually by *x*, *y*, and/or *z* angles based on its current orientation:

```
ship.runAction(SCNAction.repeatActionForever(SCNAction.
rotateByX(0, y: 2, z: 0, duration: 1)))
```

This can be broken down into its various parts, as it's an SCNAction within an SCNAction, namely, the rotateByX function wrapped into a repeatActionForever function of SCNAction. Actions in both SceneKit (SCNAction) and SpriteKit (SKAction) cannot only be added to objects by code but also in Xcode's visual editor, as we shall see later in our review of the Fox demo.

Find more on both the SCNAction and SKAction classes here:

For SCNAction, refer to https://developer.apple.com/library/ios/documentation/SceneKit/Reference/SCNAction_Class/.

For SKAction, refer to https://developer.apple.com/library/ios/documentation/SpriteKit/Reference/SKAction_Ref/.

In line (5), we create the SCNView object and assign it as the view of GameViewController with the line let scnView = self.view as! SCNView. The scene and its nodes that we created with the object named scene back in line (1) then gets assigned to the scene attribute of scnView via scnView.scene = scene. There is a slight bit of ambiguity as to which scene is assigned to what node, but this essentially has to do with the setting up of rootNode itself.

The next few lines (of (6)) show some of the properties that we can use from the SCNView class; the first being the ability to control the camera with the allowsCameraControl property. Setting this to false would prevent the player from being able to move the camera about. This could be great for in-game cut scenes or locking the camera during a part of a stage where it would be necessary. The line scnView.showsStatistics = true tells the scene to show any rendering data that would be beneficial to debugging. For example, we could see the **frames per second (fps)** our game is running at.

This is equivalent to a SpriteKit scene's code part of skView.showsFPS and skView.showsNodeCount, where skView is the name of an SKView object.

The next line, scnView.backgroundColor = UIColor.blackColor(), allows us to set the background color to black, just the same way as we did with ambientLightNode.light!.color = UIColor.darkGrayColor() using the UIColor class.

SceneKit Debugging Options

As of iOS 9, even more debugging options became available through the use of the `SCNDebugOptions` struct and the `debugOptions` attribute of `SCNView`.

If we were to write the following, we'd be able to see our ship's bounding boxes:

```
scnView.debugOptions = .ShowBoundingBoxes
```

There are other options such as `ShowLightInfluences`, `ShowPhysicsShapes`, and `ShowWireframe`.

WWDC15's Fox Demo with the .ShowBoundingBoxes and ShowPhysicsShapes options enabled

Finally, in line (7), `let tapGesture = UITapGestureRecognizer(target: self, action: "handleTap:")` creates a `UITapGestureRecognizer` object named `tapGesture`, which will call the function `handleTap(gestureRecognize: UIGestureRecognizer)` when any tap is performed and `scnView.addGestureReco gnizer(tapGesture)` adds that recognizer to the scene.

Handling user input in SceneKit

The UITapGestureRecognizer objects are great in order to selectively organize the input we receive from the player. This goes for both SceneKit and SpriteKit scenes. We can have recognizers for taps, swipes in each direction, panning, pinches, and long presses; long presses are great for when you'd need to possibly handle a character charging their attack.

Here's the documentation of the UITapGestureRecognizer class for reference:

```
https://developer.apple.com/library/prerelease/ios/documentation/
UIKit/Reference/UIGestureRecognizer_Class/index.html
```

Let's take a look at that handleTaps function as it contains an object of the SceneKit class, SCNTransaction:

```
func handleTap(gestureRecognize: UIGestureRecognizer) {
        //(1) retrieve the SCNView
        let scnView = self.view as! SCNView
        // check what nodes are tapped
        let p = gestureRecognize.locationInView(scnView)
        /(2)
        let hitResults = scnView.hitTest(p, options: nil)
        // check that we clicked on at least one object
        if hitResults.count > 0 {
            // retrieved the first clicked object
            let result: AnyObject! = hitResults[0]
            // get its material
            let material = result.node!.geometry!.firstMaterial!

        //(3)// highlight it
            SCNTransaction.begin()
            SCNTransaction.setAnimationDuration(0.5)
            // on completion - unhighlight
            SCNTransaction.setCompletionBlock {
                SCNTransaction.begin()
                SCNTransaction.setAnimationDuration(0.5)
                material.emission.contents = UIColor.blackColor()
                SCNTransaction.commit()
            }
            material.emission.contents = UIColor.redColor()
            SCNTransaction.commit()
        }
    }
```

In line (1), we are just creating a reference to the current SCNView object named scnView. Next, the constant p is created using gestureRecognize. locationInView(scnView). What this is doing is capturing the gesture's location in the view we wish to keep tabs on. In this case, it's the entire view, scnView. If we had subviews, say a game's menu screen, then we could if we'd wish only target gestures there in this fashion.

If building a game where the player has to tap at the spur of the moment and many times for a character's movement or dodging, we did find the touchesBegan() functionality we spoke about in SpriteKit to be a bit faster than UITapGestureRecognizer. This might eventually become a moot point with each new and faster iOS device, but if your game's controls are heavily dependent on quickness of the player, you might notice some lag in response to the gestures via the UITapGesterRecognizer approach. This could effect the goal of your game, so try the touchesBegan() function to see what works best for your game. Using touchesBegan() for swipes and other non-tap gestures could be rather tricky, so there's a trade-off there on the development side too.

Next in line (2), we take a count of how many of these gestures, taps in our case, were captured in the view using the hitTest() function of SCNView and only counting if that gesture made contact with any object in our scene by passing the position constant, p, as a parameter. The function hitTest() returns an array of event results, and the count property then counts how large that array is. We can then capture a reference to the first tap by referencing the first member of that array. We only have a single object in this demo provided for us, the spaceship, so we can just get an instance of Swift's most upper parent object, AnyObject. Our hitTest object, hitResults, is an array containing references to every object tapped in this context. Again, this is just our spaceship object, so we can simply take the first object instanced at hitTest[0]. This is what the result constant represents.

The line let material = result.node!.geometry!.firstMaterial! shows us how we get a reference to that object's material by drilling down the node's children using the dot operator while also implicitly unwrapping each node via the exclamation point (!). This material reference is needed for when the tap needs to make the spaceship turn red.

This is actually a nice broad example of how we can select only certain objects in our SceneKit scene to be the focus of a player's input. Here, it just picks any object using the broad type AnyObject class, but imagine a game where only a certain type of character or characters are selectable; think of an isometric top down shooter or **real-time strategy** (**RTS**) game. We could possibly check whether the tapped object only is a member of a certain class type (isKindOfClass()) or conforms to a certain protocol (conformsToProtocol()) before taking any action on those selected game objects. Want the player in your RTS game to only take actions on Tank objects? Then combining this with a menu that tells the game which object type is the focus could be what gives you that ability here in SceneKit.

In line (3), the default SceneKit template also hands us this useful bit of code showing the use of SCNTransaction. The SCNTransaction class first became available in iOS 8, and we can think of SCNTransaction as a laundry list of changes and animations we want in the scene to take place at a certain specified set of time. An SCNTransaction class begins with the SCNTransaction.begin() call and ends at the SCNTransaction.commit() call. Scene graph animation calls that are within that block get called, by default, with a 0 second delay. In many cases, we'd want to control the duration of these animations, thus we use the setAnimationDuration() function at the beginning of the SCNTransaction block to set that. The line SCNTransaction.setAnimationDuration(0.5) sets the time to complete this block at half a second. Do note that within this block is another block of code starting with SCNTransaction.setCompletionBlock{...}. What this does is execute the call only after the SCNTransation block it's within completes. In the case of this template demo, at first for half a second, the ship is highlighted red, as done in the material. emission.contents = UIColor.redColor() line. After this completes, for another half a second, the ship is brought back to it's original color by setting its material emission back to UIColor.blackColor(). This is a bit confusing at first but there are a slew of animations and transactions we can do for our scenes with this method in just one block. Check out this link to the documentation; other transitions/ transactions can be for fading in/out, camera field of view, rotation, translations, lighting, and more: https://developer.apple.com/library/prerelease/ios/ documentation/SceneKit/Reference/SCNTransaction_Class/index.html#// apple_ref/occ/clm/SCNTransaction/valueForKey.

As for the default SceneKit template, that's all the code used to make the scene. It's a basic scene and far from a game, but it should give us a basic understanding of what essentially makes up the main structure and logic of a scene in SceneKit. Before we look into the Fox demo and thus an actual full game project, let's look at a few other features that were added to Xcode as of iOS 9 / Xcode 7.

SceneKit features introduced in iOS 9 / Xcode 7

Let's go back to transitions and animations. As of iOS 9, we can change a character or other 3D object's blend mode very easily in SceneKit.

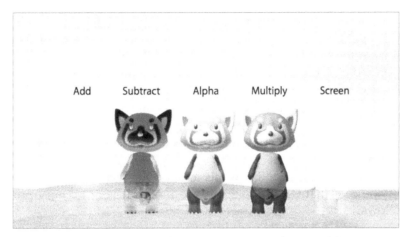

A display of the various blend modes in SceneKit from WWDC2015

Blend modes can be changed simply with one line, aSCNMaterial.blendMode = .Add, where aSCNMaterial is an object representing the material of SCNNode. Changing blend modes can create a number of effects. Some games use a player's *ghost* to show a past run through they are trying to beat, or there's the fade effect boss characters make when defeated. Combine with SCNTransaction to have characters fade in and out of these modes.

Audio nodes and 3D sound

As of iOS 9, we can place 3D sounds into our SceneKit scenes. The addAudioPlayer() function of the SCNNode class function lets us append a sound to that node, and wherever that node is in 3D space, the sound will adhere to 3D audio mixing; that is, if the audio source's positional property is set to true. Here's how we'd create 3D sound with audio nodes:

```
let source = SCNAudioSource(named: "sound.caf")
let soundEffect = SCNAudioPlayer(source: source)
node.addAudioPlayer(soundEffect)
source.positional = true
source.loops = false
```

This gives a sound effect to the game object, the SCNNode named node.

To actually play the sound, we'd need to call SCNAction on it, as shown:

```
let action = SCNAction.playAudioSource(source,
waitForCompletion: true)
node.runAction(action)
```

The waitForCompletion property makes sure that the action goes as long as the sound is. This might not be the best for a character sound effect though as you might want it stopped midway (that is, the player hits the enemy, canceling their previously started chant, yell, or something to that degree).

Ambience and music

To add music and ambience, we could follow exactly the same method as adding a sound effect to a node: create an SCNAudioSource object; add that to an SCNAudioSource object; and add this to our node with addAudioPlayer. The only difference is that we'd loop the music and set it's positional property to false as follows:

```
source.positional = false
source.loops = true
```

SpriteKit scene transitions in SceneKit

SpriteKit has some great scene transitions. We could make it look like a door is opening up or a page is turning. This could add extra character and polish to your game. Before iOS 9, we couldn't do these 2D transitions in our 3D SceneKit, but since Xcode 7 and iOS 9, we can do so in SceneKit and here's how:

```
aSCNView.presentScene(aScene, withTransition:aSKTransition,
incomingPointOfView:nil, completionHandler:nil)
```

Again, aSCNView is just a general reference to some SCNView object and when we present the scene to that view, we have the option of passing an SKTransition object for the withTransition parameter. The incomingPointOfView parameter can be a reference to a camera's point of view during the transition, and the completionHandler parameter is the name of a completion block that is called after the scene transitions. For example, we could call the functions that start the count up of our last stage's score in a score scene that was transitioned to after the stage completed. We might not want to begin the counting and other functions of the new scene until we know that the scene has been 100% transitioned to or, in this case, after we know the total points from the prior scene.

Check out some more examples of `SKTransition` on the class reference page, maybe there's a transition that could help add to your game's design:

`https://developer.apple.com/library/prerelease/ios/documentation/`
`SpriteKit/Reference/SKTransition_Ref/index.html`

Fox demo

We've been spending much of our time in both SpriteKit and here in SceneKit on the boilerplate code that makes up our game logic. As Xcode continues to update, so does the visual design features for iOS game design that don't involve a strong understanding of code. There's always some scripting involved, but one of the key features in game design is, well, the design aspect of it. At the *WWDC15* event, the introduction to iOS 9 and Xcode 7 was a great game demo that can not only teach us some of the visual design features that Xcode can do, but also gives us a beautiful start to a platforming game in SceneKit. That demo is named *Fox* and granted, though it actually stars a red panda and not a fox, we could forgive that mixup for how feature-rich and essential it can be to learn how to develop SceneKit-powered iOS games.

The Fox demo image showing our player character and level assets

There's much more to this demo than we can show here, so it's encouraged to download it for yourself and check out all of the SceneKit features it provides. We will focus on a few topics yet to be covered in either SceneKit or SpriteKit, such as particles, physics, and the scene graph. The Fox demo also makes use of 3D game/art design features, such as skyboxes, ambient occlusion, cubemap lighting, collision meshes, and more. It really is a nice-quality demo to make beautiful games in iOS.

Here is the download link provided by Apple:

```
https://developer.apple.com/library/prerelease/ios/samplecode/Fox/
Introduction/Intro.html
```

At the time of writing, the Fox demo was written only in Objective-C. We have focused on Swift in the entirety of this book, but don't worry too much if some aspects of Objective-C are foreign to you. The goal is to see the visual tools Xcode provides. In a future date, the Fox demo is bound to be available in Swift, be it by Apple themselves or by third-party programmers.

Particle systems

Some of the basic assets in any game, be it SpriteKit or SceneKit built, are the various particle effects we'd add to characters, objects, or an entire scene. Particles can add to the feel of collecting that item, give the player a signal that something is happening to the player, like they are gaining or losing health, or show the presence and power of an incoming boss fight.

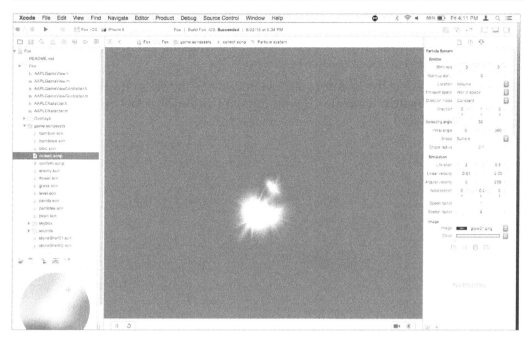

Collectable particle effect from the Fox demo

In the past, the process of making a particle effect would be to manually create sometimes rather complex particle emitter shader objects using OpenGL code. This can still be done if we so choose (using either Apple's fast, low-level API, Metal, or OpenGL), but over time, the process of visually creating and editing particle effects has gotten easier. Not too long ago in the iOS development history, frameworks such as Cocos2D/ Cocos3D allowed us to use third-party particle effects builders to import into our games. With both SpriteKit and SceneKit, Xcode as of about iOS 7/ iOS 8, a more visual representation of particles was created in Xcode thus saving us a large amount of time and effort in creating the effects we want and expect to see in our games. The image previously shown displays the Xcode particle systems editor with the Fox demo's collectable sparkle effect.

To create your own particle effect in SceneKit, follow these steps:

1. Create a new file as we did in the past by navigating to **File | New** ... or simply the keyboard shortcut *command + N*.

2. We then select the **Resource** section under iOS and select the **SceneKit Particle System** template. (If working with SpriteKit, select **SpriteKit Particle File**.)

3. Both the SpriteKit and SceneKit particle options give us a list of basic particle templates we can start from, such as Reactor, Sparkle, or Bokeh. Select one of your choosing or check out a collectable one here in the demo. For SpriteKit, this creates an SKS file and the image mask for the particles. The SceneKit template creates the 3D particle effect via an SCNP file and the image mask.

Let's take a look back at the particle system we created for the collectable particle in the demo. If not selected already, click on the attributes inspector to view various controls we can edit to customize our particle effects.

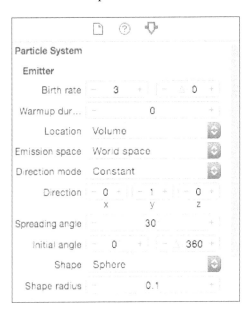

Feel free to test a number of the variables and fields within the inspector. There's the birth rate, which controls how often the particles restart their start and end animation, the image, which can make up the shape and color of the particles, and the various angles that determine the overall direction of the effects. There's also the **Looping** dropdown, which keeps the particles repeating during the life of the particle system in the scene. Additionally, the **affected by gravity** toggle is what we use to have the particles fall based on the scene's gravity. The collection particles loop constantly without gravity, and the confetti particles happen once and fall to gravity, as we'd expect confetti to behave. If an object in our scene has a physics field, we can also have the particles react to that.

Placing particles into our pioscene

When we create SpriteKit or SceneKit particles, we can call them in our scene via code in either the SpriteKit or SceneKit:

SpriteKit

SpriteKit particles aren't in the Fox demo but to backtrack a bit to our talk on SpriteKit, if we'd wanted to add particles to a 2D SpriteKit game, here's an example of how we'd accomplish that:

```
//(1)
var path = NSBundle.mainBundle().pathForResource("Spark",
ofType: "sks")
//(2)
    var sparkParticle = NSKeyedUnarchiver.
    unarchiveObjectWithFile(path!) as! SKEmitterNode
//(3)
    sparkParticle.position = CGPointMake(
    self.size.width/2, self.size.height)
    sparkParticle.name = "sparkParticle"
    sparkParticle.targetNode = self.scene
    self.addChild(sparkParticle)
```

1. We create a path to our app's bundle with the `NSBundle.mainBundle().pathForResource()` function call, and we pass the string of the particle file's name, in this case, `Spark`, with the file type, SKS.

2. Next, we create the `sparkParticle` object using the `NSKeyedUnarchiver.unarchiveObjectWithFile(path!)` call that, as we see, takes the path we created in part `(1)`. It's casted as the particle object for SpriteKit, `SKEmitterNode`. `NSKeyedUnarchiver` is a class used to decode named objects from keyed archives, an encoded hierarchy of archives. This class has some support of what is known type coercion. In short, it can decode objects in files, be it whether in a 32-bit or 64-bit architecture. More on this special file decoding class here: `https://developer.apple.com/library/mac/documentation/Cocoa/Reference/Foundation/Classes/NSKeyedUnarchiver_Class/`

3. We then set a position and name for this particle effect and target it to the scene while also adding it to the scene node.

Though this example isn't given in the Fox demo, this is a great example of how we can target specific files in our project's navigation hierarchy.

SceneKit

SceneKit particles are members of the `SCNParticleSystem` class. We add these particles to our scene with the `addParticleSystem` function of the `SCNNode` class. The Fox demo does this in the `collectFlower()` function with the following Objective-C line:

```
[self.gameView.scene addParticleSystem:_collectParticles
withTransform:particlePosition];
```

What this code is doing is calling the scene in the designated view and adding the particles, which are declared earlier in the class as `_collectParticles` to our scene. It then tells the scene at which point in space this effect will appear. In this case, it's the `particalPosition` variable that when traced back is taken from the `SCNNode` parameter passed into the `collectFlower()` function.

Here's how this would be written in Swift:

```
scene.particleEmitNode.addParticleSystem(_
    collectable!)
```

Swift's `addParticleSystem` API unfortunately doesn't have the `withTransform` parameter as in Objective-C, so we'd have to add the particle system to the node it will be emitting from, which is denoted by the `particleEmitNode` variable. This most likely will change in future API changes of Swift 2.x and later.

Introducing SceneKit and SpriteKit physics

When we look at the `collectFlower()` function from our particle example, we see that there's an `SCNNode` parameter passed. This node comes from the function `physicsWorld`. In both SpriteKit and SceneKit, we can create an overall set of physics rules and handle various physics-related interactions, most notably, contacts between two or more nodes. One of the most basic aspects of any game is to do something when game objects hit each other. This could be when the player touches a collectable, when enemies contact the player or the player hits the enemy with an attack. In iOS development and in game engines, we call these boundaries between 2D sprites or 3D objects as bounding boxes. We mentioned these physics objects briefly in our talk of iOS 9 and later `debugOptions` property. Bounding boxes for SceneKit objects are created automatically based on the simplified version of an object's geometry, but we can edit these shapes with the `SCNBoundingVolume` class.

More documentation of this class can be found at `https://developer.apple.com/library/prerelease/ios/documentation/SceneKit/Reference/SCNBoundingVolume_Protocol/index.html`.

Game physics in iOS and game development in general are much larger topics than we can discuss in this chapter. So for now, let's just see how the Fox demo and iOS games in general handle the simple concept of two nodes contacting their bounding boxes.

```
func physicsWorld(world: SCNPhysicsWorld, didUpdateContact
contact: SCNPhysicsContact) {
if (contact.nodeA.physicsBody.categoryBitMask ==
AAPLBitmaskSuperCollectable) {
        self.collectFlower(contact.nodeA)
    }
if (contact.nodeB.physicsBody.categoryBitMask ==
AAPLBitmaskSuperCollectable) {
        self.collectFlower(contact.nodeB)
    }
}
```

Preceding is a Swift pseudo code example of the Fox demo's `physicsWorld` function. The function takes in two parameters, `world` of the type `SCNPhysicsWorld` that represents the entire physics environment of a scene and the object representing the physics contact of the type `SCNPhysicsContact`. The function here checks the bitmask of the nodes in the contact. If the first or second node of the contact (`nodeA` or `nodeB`) are in the flower's specific category, then the `collectFlower()` function is called and that collectable's node is passed as a parameter.

Bitmasking is when we designate a set of bits for another set of bits that can be combined together using bitwise math. Think of it as using 1s and 0s to not only categorize a range of ones and zeros but also allow us to handle situations where many categories happen in the same context.

For example, we have different categories of objects/events in our game and we fit them in their own *slots* in a byte (8 bits). In the Fox demo, the game collisions are a bitshift value of 2, thus they represent 00000100 in binary. The *category designation* of collectables in the Fox demo a bitshift of 3 or 00001000, the enemies are 4, 00010000.

In the demo, we see the following code for `AAPLBitmaskSuperCollectable`:

```
// Collision bit masks
typedef NS_OPTIONS(NSUInteger, AAPLBitmask) {
    AAPLBitmaskCollision        = 1UL << 2,
    AAPLBitmaskCollectable      = 1UL << 3,
    AAPLBitmaskEnemy            = 1UL << 4,
```

```
    AAPLBitmaskSuperCollectable = 1UL << 5,
    AAPLBitmaskWater            = 1UL << 6
};
```

When the category bitmask in either `nodeA` or `nodeB` of the collision match the flower collectable (if the *slot* is *on* per say, or equal to 1, then we know the collectable was involved in the collision).

Swift version 1 didn't really have a similar way to mimic bitmasking as done in Objective-C with NSOptions, but as of Swift 2.0, we can perform bitmasking like the demo in the following way:

```
struct AAPLBitmask : AAPLBitmaskType {
  let rawValue: Int
  init(rawValue: Int) { self.rawValue = rawValue }

  static var None: AAPLBitmaskType { return
  AAPLBitmask(rawValue: 0) }
  static var AAPLBitmaskCollision : AAPLBitmask
{ return AAPLBitmask(rawValue: 1 << 2) }
  static var AAPLBitmaskCollectable : AAPLBitmask
{ return AAPLBitmask(rawValue: 1 << 3) }
  static var AAPLBitmaskEnemy : AAPLBitmask
{ return AAPLBitmask(rawValue: 1 << 4) }
static var AAPLBitmaskSuperCollectable : AAPLBitmask
{ return AAPLBitmask(rawValue: 1 << 5) }
static var AAPLBitmaskWater : AAPLBitmask
{ return AAPLBitmask(rawValue: 1 << 6) }
}
```

Essentially, it's a struct that returns bitshifted static variables of itself. It's not as elegant as seen in Objective-C and in past C implementation, but if we wish to use bitmasking in boilerplate code in Swift, this should allow you to do so.

One last note about the `physicsWorld()` function, in order for the function to be called during the collision of two physics bodies, we need to set the physics world delegate. In most cases, that delegate would be the current game scene.

```
scene.physicsWorld.contactDelegate = self
```

Xcode will most likely tell you that a physics world delegate wasn't set and if you haven't, this is the code that is usually placed in the `viewDidLoad()` function of `ViewController`.

Visually composed game scenescgs

Getting back to the visual aspects of the Fox demo, let's look at the game scene objects created in the project and how we can view the nodes in what's known as the **scene graph**.

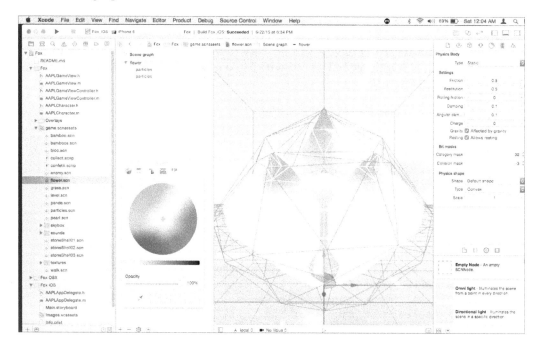

We see that game objects and particle effects in the Fox demo can be visually manipulated in Xcode and together in one view. The preceding image shows the flower collectable and its components that consist of the 3D mesh, lighting, bounding boxes, and the particle effects. In SceneKit, we do this with a SceneKit scene file (SCN).

To view the scene's scene graph, click on the side window icon found toward the bottom-left of the Xcode window under the visual editor window of the scene, as seen in the following screenshot:

This is a screenshot of the scene graph. Those familiar with the game engines, such as Unity and Unreal Engine, will be quite familiar with this type of component/game scene view. The scene graph shows the dropdown hierarchy of all the objects in the scene including their own internal components. The flower power-up consists of a 3D mesh model named *flower* that has two child particle effects as well as a physics body. All three are denoted by the three symbols seen on the right-hand side of the graph's objects.

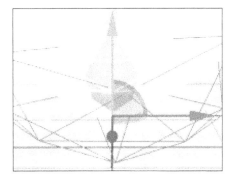

We can move the model around in the scene, using X, Y, and Z markers seen in the preceding image. We can also zoom in, zoom out, rotate the scene, as well as add more objects to the scene.

To add more objects to the scene, follow these:

1. Go to the **media library** found in the library windows at the bottom-right of the screen (seen in the prior image).

2. Now search for `grass` and simply drag and drop it into the scene. Now the premade grass object is in this scene as a reference.

3. This is actually how the `level.scn` file was composed.

4. There's also the option to add primitive objects to the scene and build them up from there, which is again very similar to the design-centric game engines. Simply select from the object library tab right next to the media library icon and search `geometry`. There are primitive objects, such as spheres, planes, and boxes.

5. The primitive objects lack the lighting, materials and other details that we can see in the grass and other premade objects in the projects. Use the even more detailed inspector windows for these objects to see and edit various details, such as the physics bodies, materials, baking the lighting, and object name identification for any scripting/coding.

6. There's also actions that can be added to these objects. Click on the secondary editor icon (the upside down triangle in a square at the button right of the flow scene's view). This will open the secondary editor that shows a `RotateByEuler` action if the flower asset is selected in the scene graph.

7. What this action does is rotate the flower once every second. To see this in action, click on the Play button seen just above the secondary editor window timeline. We can see how this object will rotate from this action.

8. The action can be shortened or extended by expanding or condensing it in the secondary editor timeline. More details about the action can be edited in the Inspector window, and if we'd like, we can use the library to add more actions to this object or remove the one provided to have it act in a different way.

Test out a few actions, times, and properties yourself. We can see how, without any code, we can set up a scene visually and dynamically control actions of each object in that scene. Many of these visual features and actions work for both SceneKit and SpriteKit scenes.

Look at the `level.scn` file to see a scene with a fully composed level camera object (as seen in the previous screenshot). Do you want to make a similar level with maybe more obstacles and a different skybox? Copy the level and change those assets and name it `level2`. This can save a monumental amount of time in the design of games and levels. From Xcode 7 onwards, we have tools directly in the IDE that originally were only for the multiplatform game engines. It really puts the design back into game design.

Much of the manual code we've gone over could get daunting, especially for those of us who may want to get into game design but are still relatively new to coding.

```
//Objective-C
SCNScene *scene = [SCNScene
sceneNamed:@"game.scnassets/level.scn"];
//Swift
let scene = SCNScene(named: "game.scnassets/level.scn")!
```

This is all we need to reference a scene from the visually designed tools. Add it to the view's root node like we spoke about in the SceneKit basic template and it's ready to go. Use code to add spawning enemies, the player, and the 2D SpriteKit overlay (which can itself have actions and visual designs in its SKS file), and it's a full-fledged game.

For more information on the SceneKit framework as well as the latest updates and additions to its library, see the full documentation link as follows:

```
https://developer.apple.com/library/ios/documentation/SceneKit/
Reference/SceneKit_Framework/
```

Summary

At the start of this chapter, we first spoke briefly about the history of 3D game design in iOS and how SceneKit came to be from the necessity to have a first-party, dynamically robust framework aimed at the complexities of 3D game development. We then went over the basic structure of SceneKit and how it and SpriteKit from the previous chapter work off the concept of nodes, starting from the view and moving on to the scene node and child nodes in that scene. Next, we went over how SpriteKit and SceneKit can be used together in the same scene as we then moved on to dissecting the default SceneKit template given to us in Xcode, and its various assets. In addition to a review of template project's code, we also reviewed some of the features, code, and assets, such as the audio nodes, lend modes, and debug options that became available as of iOS 9 / Xcode 7. Finally, for the remainder of the chapter, we spoke much about the Fox demo shown during the *WWDC15* convention and the various visual game design features that became available since the announcement of Xcode 7.

For our next chapter, we will go into the features of the GameplayKit framework, which we introduced briefly when we went over the benefits of using composite-based structuring when building our games. With GameplayKit, we can duplicate and reuse premade game actions and rules as we did here in this chapter with the visual components of our games.

5
GameplayKit

For many years, video game development has relied on the tenets of **object-oriented design** (**OOD**). Of the core features in OOD, the concepts of inheritance and polymorphism have been the most useful in this branch of software engineering. It makes sense to think of entities in our games as homogenous groups of objects; objects that we then write rules for in how they interact with each other. For example, thanks to inheritance, all objects in our game can be given the class name of `GameObject`; they have functions we'll use throughout the game and then we can branch them off into child classes, such as `Player` or `Enemy`. We can then continue that thought process as we come up with more specific types of entities, be they objects such as `Player`, different enemies, **non-player characters** (**NPCs**), or whatever makes sense for the game we are making. Calling a function on those objects, such as `Shoot()` or `Health()`, could be unique for each child of the parent class and thus we make use of polymorphism in OOD.

However, as mentioned in the previous chapter, although inheritance-based structuring is great for most software applications (including simple games), the unique needs and pairings of video game rules and entities cause inheritance-based structuring to break one of the rules of OOP. That rule is the reusability of our code. The solution to that problem is to separate the game objects and the game's rules into what's known as component-based structuring. Building games with this mentality can allow us to build unique objects, actions, and rules with the ability to not only shift them around throughout our single game project, but also to use them in other projects, cutting the overly customized structuring in which building a game via inheritance-based structuring can cause.

Apple's solution to this issue is the GameplayKit framework. GameplayKit is a completely independent framework that can be used with both SpriteKit or SceneKit games, as well as games written in low-level APIs, such as OpenGL and Metal. First announced for iOS 9 and Xcode 7 at *WWDC15*, GameplayKit takes the common methodologies and concepts used in game development for years and allows us to work on those aspects independently of what is being drawn on the screen. This framework doesn't handle what's drawn on the screen and is, thus, made specifically for the Model portion of MVC.

There are several game development concepts handled by GameplayKit, which we shall review in this chapter. These concepts are **entities and components**, **state machines**, **agents**, **goals**, **behaviors**, pathfinding, MinMaxAI, random sources, and rule systems.

Entities and components

We can think of entities as the objects in our game. They can be the player, an enemy character, an NPC, level decorations and backgrounds, or even the UI used to inform the player of their lives, power, and other stats. The entity is thought of as a container of components. Components are behaviors that dictate the appearance and actions of an entity. One might ask, "how is this any different from objects and functions?" The short answer is that objects and functions in inheritance-based design describe more of what our game objects are, while working with component-based structuring focuses more on what they do. As we deal with the classes and functionality of the GameplayKit framework, we will be able to get a better handle on this. In this framework, we'll see that entities and components are handled with the GKEntity and GKComponent classes, respectively.

 If you are still a bit confused about component-based structuring, check back in our previous chapter where we went into this in a bit more detail. You can also visit the developer page about this design methodology here: https://developer.apple.com/library/prerelease/ios/documentation/General/Conceptual/GameplayKit_Guide/EntityComponent.html.

Using GKEntity and GKComponent objects in our games

Anyone familiar with Java or C# will understand the concept of an *abstract* class. The GKComponent class is essentially an abstract class. Quoting from the speakers at WWDC: think of components as "little black boxes of functionality." Objects of the class GKEntity are like our generic GameObject class mentioned before. However, unlike the objects we've dealt with before, we typically don't add too much in the way of custom functionality to them (otherwise, we'd be leaning towards inheritance-based structuring).

We first create a game object and subclass it as a member of the GKEntity type. For this example, let's just call our object class GameEntity. Also, don't forget to import the GameplayKit API:

```
import GameplayKit
class GameEntity : GKEntity
```

Again, our goal with an object of the type GKEntity is to use it as a container for GKComponent objects. Objects of the GKEntity class inherit the following functions:

- components: This is a property that returns an array of the GKComponents in our GKEntity object

- addComponent(_:): This is a function that we use to add GKComponents to our GKEntity

- removeComponentForClass(_:): This removes a component for a class of GKEntity objects

- updateWithDeltaTime(_:): This updates with the render/game loop for each component in the entity; this is what's known as per-entity updating

The last function in the GKEntity class, updateWithDeltaTime(_:), is one of the two mechanisms used by GameplayKit when dispatching updates to our game object's components. The update mechanisms are as follows:

- **Per-entity**: This is good for updating smaller game structures without causing lag. The updateWithDeltaTime(_:) function of GKEntity calls all of the entity objects' updateWithDeltaTime(_:) functions and then dispatches that to all of the component's updateWithDeltaTime(_:) functions.

- **Per-component**: This is made for larger projects and more complex game logic. When updating via the per-component mechanism, we use the class type GKComponentSystem to categorize groups of components and then call its updateWithDeltaTime(_:) function to fire off updates specific to the class of component instances it manages. GKComponentSystem doesn't make note of your game's entity/component hierarchy, so they can be used to efficiently update more complex games.

For example, if we have a specific way we want to update player and enemy *attacks*, then we create an object of the GKComponentSystem class, initiate it with the initWithComponentClass(_:) function, and pass that class of components (in this case, *Attack* components) to that system. It's in that GKComponentSystem object's updateWithDeltaTime(_:) function that we specify the unique update logic for that group of components, independently of the entity updates. This can come in handy when dealing with enemy/NPC AI in more complex games.

Here's a visual look at these classes:

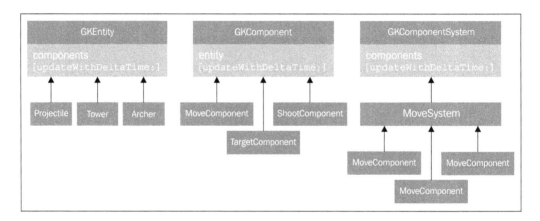

Don't worry if this is still somewhat confusing. Those of you who may be more familiar with the game engine Unity will have seen how components, such as rigid bodies, materials, and scripts, can be added to objects placed in a game scene. The concept here with iOS components and entities is not that much different. Each component in Unity and other engines can be its own independently working functionality.

Let's take a look at the code snippet provided during the *WWDC15* conference, in both Objective-C and Swift, showing how we'd create entities, components, and component systems in our projects:

```
//Objective-C
/* Make our archer */
GKEntity *archer = [GKEntity entity];
/* Archers can move, shoot, be targeted */
[archer addComponent: [MoveComponent component]];
[archer addComponent: [ShootComponent component]];
[archer addComponent: [TargetComponent component]];
/* Create MoveComponentSystem */
GKComponentSystem *moveSystem =
        [GKComponentSystem
        systemWithComponentClass:MoveComponent.class];
/* Add archer's MoveComponent to the system */
[moveSystem addComponent: [archer
componentForClass:MoveComponent.class]];

//Swift
/* Make our archer */
let archer = GKEntity()
/* Archers can move, shoot, be targeted */
let moveComponent = MoveComponent()
let shootComponent = ShootComponent()
let targetComponent = TargetComponent()

archer.addComponent(moveComponent)
archer.addComponent(shootComponent)
archer.addComponent(targetComponent)

/* Create MoveComponentSystem */
let moveComponentSystem = GKComponentSystem(componentClass:
MoveComponent.self)

/* Add archer's MoveComponent to the system */
moveComponentSystem.addComponent(archer.
componentForClass(MoveComponent.self)!)
```

What this code does is create our `GKEntity` objects; in this case, the tower game example's archer character. Next it adds predefined `GKComponent` objects via the `addComponent(_:)` function. We also create a `GKComponentSystem` object named `moveComponentSystem` that will be used to update only movement type components. The archer's own `moveComponent` class is added to this system with `moveComponentSystem.addComponent(_:)`. Make a note of how the parameters passed through this object in addition to its initialization are class types of the component types denoted by the `.class` or `.self` properties, depending on which language we are writing our code in.

As of this publication, the `componentForClass()` function might not be fully functional for the Swift programming language. So if the Swift implementation isn't working as expected for this and other GameplayKit object initializations, the Objective-C version of this code will need to be used and linked to your project via an Objective-C–Swift bridging file. This will more than likely be ironed out in future updates to Swift as Apple continues to move away from Objective-C as the main language of the platform. For more information on how to make this bridging file, check out this link: `https://developer.apple.com/library/ios/documentation/Swift/Conceptual/BuildingCocoaApps/MixandMatch.html`.

Apple provides us with a project named `Maze` that uses these classes as well as some other concepts we'll be going over shortly.

Here's a link to the project that could help to give you an even better idea of entities and components:

`https://developer.apple.com/sample-code/wwdc/2015/downloads/Maze.zip`

Before we go over more specific code use related to `GKEntity` and `GKComponent` objects, we'll look into a game development concept that is best coupled with these objects, which is the concept of **state machines**.

State machines

A video game, more than any other type of application, bases much of its logic on whether the game or entities in that game are currently in one of a number of different states.

This could be checking whether the game is in the *intro* scene, running in the main gameplay mode, the player has died, the player is idle, a boss enemy has appeared, the game is over, the stage is over, the boss is low on health, and much more.

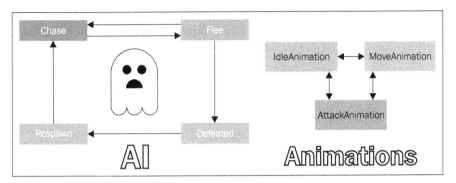

An example of state machines for either AI or character animations

In the past, it has always been common practice for game developers to write their own custom state machine logic from scratch and then use the update/render cycle to check on these various states. Typically this would be done in a custom class or simply in a custom-made enum object that will shift through various states, such as `.GameOver`, `.MainGame`, `.LowHealth`, and so on. These states could also describe the status of an individual entity in our game and dictate which animation cycle to run. For example, the player could be charging their attack and we'd want to use that state of the player to animate the charging animation. Objects in the game scene might check back on such states via switch statements to make sure that they are not doing any action that wouldn't make sense based on the context of the state. It wasn't too long before multiplatform game engines made this a part of the workflow, particularly in the animation handlers. These objects that let us inform the game and entities in the game of the various states are known as state machines. GameplayKit allows us to work with this concept in conjunction with its component/entity functionality. The framework provides the abstract class `GKState` for us to subclass from for our game's states, and the class `GKStateMachine` to utilize for placing these state objects into a designated state machine. An object of the type `GKStateMachine` can only be in one state at a time, so it gives us a better way to use and reuse these states, as opposed to the old boilerplate/switch statement methodology.

The previous diagram is from *WWDC15* and uses an example of what a PacMan-like ghost character's, or any other game character's, animation and AI state machines would look like. Also note that not all paths could lead to each other. For example, the ghost can switch back and forth between chasing and fleeing, but can neither be defeated while chasing nor could it respawn unless it was previously in the defeated state. These are known as state transitions or edges in a state machine.

By default, all edges are valid and we override the isValidNextState(_:) function in our GKState objects/components to tell the state machine if we are allowed to move between certain states.

Here's how this is done in the DemoBots sample program's TaskBotAgentControlledState class. DemoBots is the iOS 9 SpriteKit demo mentioned in *Chapter 3*, *SpriteKit and 2D Game Design*:

```
override func isValidNextState(stateClass: AnyClass) -> Bool {
        switch stateClass {
            case is FlyingBotPreAttackState.Type, is
            GroundBotRotateToAttackState.Type, is
            TaskBotZappedState.Type:
                return true
            default:
                return false
        }
    }
```

This tells the state machine that the TaskBotAgentControlledState state can transition to FlyingBotPreAttackState, GroundBotRotateToAttackState, or TaskBotZappedState. This object is another of the GameplayKit component type known as an **Agent** (which we will go over next), but for now note how we validate which transitions can happen in the isValidNextState() function.

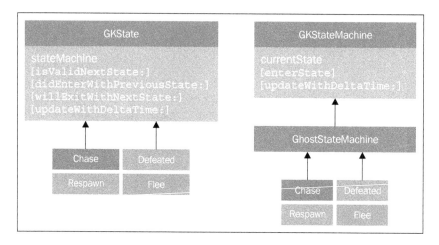

Here we see a visual representation of the GKState and GKStateMachine classes. As stated before, isValidNextState() tells us which state transitions are valid. The didEnterWithPreviousState() function is where we tell our components what to do when the state is entered, and the willExitWithNextState() function is where we tell the component(s) what to do when the state is exiting to the next state. The updateWithDeltaTime() function, as with previously mentioned GameplayKit objects, is where we put our render/game loop cycle updates. Optionally, we can also add more functionality to these classes through inheritance. For example, we can create a previousState property to collect more information about the prior state. We can then potentially use that information for our own helper functions, such as exitState() or execute().

Here's a code snippet showing how to create state machines and how to add GKState objects to them:

```
/* Make some states - Chase, Flee, Defeated, Respawn */
let chase = ChaseState()
let flee  = FleeState()
let defeated = DefeatedState()
let respawn  = RespawnState()
/* Create a state machine */
let stateMachine = GKStateMachine(states:
[chase,flee,defeated,respawn])
/* Enter our initial state - Chase */
stateMachine.enterState(chase.classForCoder)
```

In the preceding code, we see the states created from the premade classes of GKState (chase, flee, defeated, and respawn). The stateMachine object, at initialization, receives a parameter of an array of GKState objects, as shown in: let stateMachine = GKStateMachine(states: [chase,flee,defeated,respawn]). Then, in this example, we start that state machine at the state chase. This, of course, will be different based on the logic of your own game's components. GKStateMachine objects can also return the currentState() function; thus, we can guide various entities and components in our game based on the current pulse of the game's objects.

Find out more on GKState and GKStateMachine in the following full documentation:

- https://developer.apple.com/library/prerelease/ios/
  documentation/GameplayKit/Reference/GKState_Class/
- https://developer.apple.com/library/prerelease/ios/
  documentation/GameplayKit/Reference/GKStateMachine_Class/index.
  html#//apple_ref/occ/instm/GKStateMachine/canEnterState

Next we go over agents, goals, and behaviors.

Agents, goals, and behaviors

When we make entities in our games, particularly those that are not the player, we want them to perform various actions. These actions are dictated by **artificial intelligence** (**AI**) that we give them, and are based on various states of the game, the player, the environment, or the player themselves. We can have a group of enemies follow a certain path, track the player, or automatically move smoothly around obstacles using our game's physical world. The framework allows us to make our game entities be what's known as **agents**. Agents are entities that can have goals and behaviors attached to them.

Agents in GameplayKit, which utilize the `GKAgent` class, can have `GKComponent` objects that automatically set various behaviors and are based on the weight of their goals. The weight of a goal is usually a float from `0` to `1`. The higher the goal's weight value is compared with other goals, the greater the chance that the agent will perform those behaviors. For example, if an enemy character is low on health, we'd probably want their `Heal` goal to have a higher goal weight. The enemy will behave in a fashion that shows the urgency of that current low health situation by healing more often and thus giving the player a more challenging and intelligent opponent. In other words, agents, goals, and behaviors are a stackable and malleable AI system.

Here's an overview of this functionality in GameplayKit:

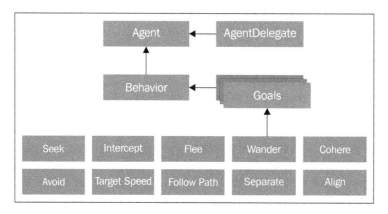

A behavior, via the `GKBehavior` class, is made of an array of `GKGoal` objects that are each given a certain weight. For example, we could have a `GKBehavior` class for an NPC in a racing game named `RacingBehavior`. That behavior would be a combination of two goals, such as `FollowPath` and `AvoidAgents`. Together those goals would make a character in our game that will automatically move away from other NPCs while staying on the current track for the stage we are in.

Here's a visual representation of these classes:

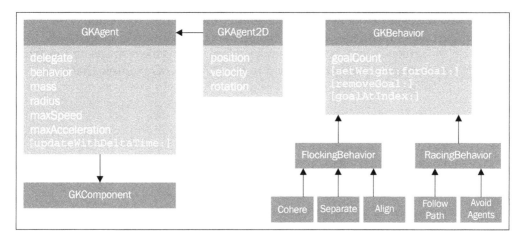

A GKAgent object, as we can see in the preceding image, has a number of physics-based properties, such as mass, radius, maxSpeed, and more. Like other GameplayKit objects, it utilizes the updateWithDeltaTime() function to sync with the render/game loop updates of either GKComponentSystem or GKEntity. Are you starting to see a pattern here with these objects? In a way, we can also think of a GKAgent object being similar to a SpriteKit or a SceneKit node since they work on our game's physics. However, whether we made our game with SpriteKit, SceneKit, or our own custom render components, such as in OpenGL or Metal, we need to link up these classes to what's displayed on the screen with the special GKAgentDelegate class. Here's a diagram of that class and its functions:

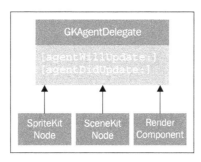

The `agentWillUpdate()` function is what we use to tell the agent what to do just before the game's `update()` function, and the `agentDidUpdate()` function is what we use to tell the agent what to do on screen after the `update()` function. This can be, in the case of a `Follow` `GKGoal` object, having a reference to the player's position on the screen before the update takes place. Here's the example of this from *WWDC15*, but written in Swift as opposed to the Objective-C example that was given:

```
func agentWillUpdate(agent:GKAgent)
{
    /* Position the agent to match our sprite */
     agent.position = self.position
     agent.rotation = self.zRotation
}
func agentDidUpdate(agent:GKAgent)
{
    /* Position the sprite to match our agent */
     self.position = agent.position
     self.zRotation = agent.zRotation
}
```

Let's look at an example to see what a `GKGoal`/`GKAgent` interaction looks like. Here's a code snippet found in the DemoBot project's `TaskBotBehavior.swift` class, which is a child of `GKBehavior`:

```
// (1)
let separationGoal = GKGoal(toSeparateFromAgents:
agentsToFlockWith, maxDistance:
GameplayConfiguration.Flocking.separationRadius, maxAngle:
GameplayConfiguration.Flocking.separationAngle)
// (2)

behavior.setWeight(GameplayConfiguration.Flocking.
separationWeight, forGoal: separationGoal)
```

In line `(1)`, the `toSeparateFromAgents` parameter of `GKGoal` lets us pass a reference for the `GKAgent` objects we wish to keep a certain distance from.

In line `(2)`, the `behavior.setWeight()` function passes the predetermined float `GameplayConfiguration.Flocking.separationWeight` as the weight for this very goal. The higher the weight, the more priority is put on that goal.

You'll notice from the full documentation of GKGoal linked to later that much of the GKGoal class deals with the attraction or repulsion agents have to each other. Combining different characteristics of this basic functionality lets us create unique goals that GKAgent parameters get, as shown here: https://developer.apple.com/ library/prerelease/ios/documentation/GameplayKit/Reference/GKGoal_ Class/index.html.

To backtrack a bit, here is a more basic way we can create these objects, as shown at the conference both in Objective-C and Swift.

```
//Objective-C
/* Make some goals, we want to seek the enemy, avoid
obstacles, target speed */
GKGoal *seek = [GKGoal goalToSeekAgent:enemyAgent];
GKGoal *avoid = [GKGoal goalToAvoidObstacles:obstacles];
GKGoal *targetSpeed = [GKGoal goalToReachTargetSpeed:50.0f];
/* Combine goals into behavior */
GKBehavior *behavior = [GKBehavior
behaviorWithGoals:@[seek,avoid,targetSpeed]
    andWeights:@[@1.0,@5.0,@0.5]];
/* Make an agent - add the behavior to it */
GKAgent2D *agent = [[GKAgent2D* alloc] init];
agent.behavior = behavior;

//Swift
/* Make some goals, we want to seek the enemy, avoid obstacles,
target speed */
let seek  = GKGoal(toSeekAgent: enemyAgent)
let avoid = GKGoal(toAvoidObstacles: obstacles,
maxPredictionTime: 0.5)
let targetSpeed = GKGoal(toReachTargetSpeed: 50.0)
/* Combine goals into behavior */
let behavior = GKBehavior(goals: [seek, avoid, targetSpeed],
andWeights: [1.0, 5.0, 0.5])
/* Make an agent - add the behavior to it */
let agent = GKAgent2D()
agent.behavior = behavior
```

We see in the preceding code that when we create goals we assign agents to them that we are either seeking or avoiding. Goals on agents can have a target speed, as seen with the toReachTargetSpeed: parameter, and these can all be bundled up into the current behavior with set weights given to them.

Here's more documentation on GKGoal, GKAgent, GKAgentDelegate, and GKBehavior:

https://developer.apple.com/library/prerelease/ios/documentation/General/Conceptual/GameplayKit_Guide/Agent.html

One other thing to note is that the obstacles array reference passed here is part of the GKObstacle class. This class references objects on the scene that we tell agents to usually avoid when moving across the screen, and are part of our next topic, **Pathfinding**.

Pathfinding

Navigation is an integral part of most games. We could have an overworld scene in our game showing the various levels traversed or yet to be visited, with branching pathways to each point, or we could have a 3D action platformer with a spell that points out a logical path to our next quest or battle location. We can also see pathfinding in top-down isometric games. For instance, the player could be fighting off a hoard of enemies all locked on the player's location on the screen. Good pathfinding AI would not only tell the enemies to move toward their goal, but to dynamically avoid any impassable objects in their way and detour to a better route automatically . In our talk on agents, goals, and behaviors, we somewhat covered that. Behaviors, which GKAgent objects adhere to, sync with various game physics and thus create smooth AI movements to change with other agents/objects in the scene. However, it would be great to also be able to inform these components where they can and can't traverse in a scene, and that's where pathfinding comes in.

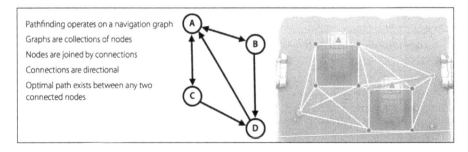

The preceding diagram shows what Pathfinding is and is an in-game visual given to us by Apple during the *WWDC15* conference. It can be broken down as follows:

- Pathfinding involves nodes with transversal paths to and from those nodes in what's known as a **navigation graph**.

- These nodes can be single directional or bidirectional and, most importantly, there can be a path calculated with this graph that represents the best path a GKAgent can take.

- The squares shown in the earlier scene represent GKObstacle objects that are placed in the scene (be it by code or visually in the Xcode editor's tools).

Here's the full documentation for the GKObstacle class:

https://developer.apple.com/library/prerelease/ios/documentation/
GameplayKit/Reference/GKObstacle_Class/index.html

Like other GameplayKit features, we use various abstract classes to child from for setting up the navigation graph and overall Pathfinding functionality; those classes are GKGraph, GKGridGraph, GKGridGraphNode, and GKObstacleGraph.

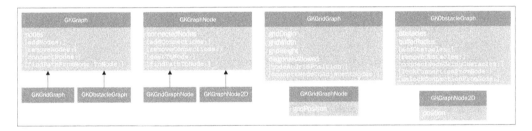

It's not too foreboding when we see the preceding diagram of classes and go through them one by one. The main, and most common, class used id the GKGraph class. This is where we can attach to it one of two different graph specification types: GKGridGraph or GKObstacleGraph. GKGraph lets us add and remove nodes, connect them, and find the optimal path between nodes. Of the two specification types, GKGridGraph has a simpler functionality that is meant for easy, 2D-based navigation graph creation, whereas GKObstacleGraph lets us set up a navigation graph using GKObstacle objects. Nodes are automatically created around those obstacles based on their shape, and these classes do much of the footwork needed to calculate the paths our agents need to take from the start to the finish of their set path(s). If we want to add even more functionality to our nodes, say if we want customized movement based on terrain type in addition to shape, then we could use the nodes of GridGraphNode.

The costToNode() function, for example, can be used to indicate that though this path would be the optimal path on a flat, even and similar type plane, it would cost more to traverse. For example, if there's quicksand in our game, the player could traverse it, so it wouldn't make sense to make an impassable GKObstacle object over the quicksand. Instead we would say that the path across that terrain between the two nodes costs more. This will make our game's navigation smarter and will handle such custom parameters.

The costToNode() function is actually an example of best practice. We can choose to not use it, but, if we are not careful, our game's pathfinding AI could end up rather unintuitive. This would not only make a poor experience for the player, but end up adding more time from debugging faulty AI actions later on.

Let's look at some code samples to get a better understanding of these classes and how to work with them. Do note that the code as of *WWDC15* is in Objective-C.

```
/* Make an obstacle - a simple square */
vector_float2 points[] = {{400,400}, {500,400}, {500,500},
{400,500}};
GKPolygonObstacle *obstacle = [[GKPolygonObstacle alloc]
initWithPoints:points count:4];
/* Make an obstacle graph */
GKObstacleGraph *graph = [GKObstacleGraph graphWithObstacles:@
[obstacle] bufferRadius:10.0f];
/* Make nodes for hero position and destination */
GKGraphNode2D *startNode = [GKGraphNode2D
nodeWithPoint:hero.position];
GKGraphNode2D *endNode = [GKGraphNode2D
nodeWithPoint:goalPosition];
/* Connect start and end node to graph */
[graph connectNodeUsingObstacles:startNode];
[graph connectNodeUsingObstacles:endNode];
/* Find path from start to end */
NSArray *path = [graph findPathFromNode:startNode toNode:endNode];
```

This code snippet uses the functionality of GKObstacleGraph by first manually creating 2D vector points in the points array and initializing the GKObstacleGraph object and graph with those points. Next, the two GKGraphNode2D objects are created to represent the start and end nodes for a hero character in the game. Then, finally, the optimal path for that hero character is created and stored into the array automatically; that is, a path using the graph's findpathFromNode: and toNode: parameters using the startNode and endNode objects, respectively. This path object can then be used in our hero's movement component or may be a map visual component to move to or indicate to the player the correct path needed to traverse the game stage's obstacles.

The following code sample is how the DemoBots project worked with the navigation in Swift, using what's known as a lazy stored property.

More information on the Swift keyword, lazy, can be found here:

https://developer.apple.com/library/ios/documentation/Swift/
Conceptual/Swift_Programming_Language/Properties.html

Swift example from DemoBots:

```
lazy var graph: GKObstacleGraph = GKObstacleGraph(obstacles:
self.polygonObstacles, bufferRadius: GameplayConfiguration.
TaskBot.pathfindingGraphBufferRadius)

lazy var obstacleSpriteNodes: [SKSpriteNode] =
self["world/obstacles/*"] as! [SKSpriteNode]
/*the above line casts the obstacles in our project's
"world/obstacles/" folder path as an implicitly unwrapped
array of SKSpriteNodes
*/

lazy var polygonObstacles: [GKPolygonObstacle] =
SKNode.obstaclesFromNodePhysicsBodies(self.obstacleSpriteNodes)
```

In short, lazy variables are quick array initializations in which their values are not known at first and are controlled by outside sources. In the case of DemoBots, these are obstacles that are created automatically from the bounds of SpriteKit nodes, which is done by the SpriteKit node function obstaclesFromNodePhysicsBodies(). This example, just shows how much time can be saved when using the provided frameworks. In the first example and more so in past game development, much of this logic would have to be manually done via terribly complex boilerplate code logic.

For more information on Pathfinding with GameplayKit, check out the examples and documentation found here:

```
https://developer.apple.com/library/prerelease/ios/documentation/
General/Conceptual/GameplayKit_Guide/Pathfinding.html
```

MinMaxAI

So far, we've created AI that's great for the components and objects that are active in a scene with their movement, behaviors, and navigation, but what about AI that can understand the game's rules like the player? A good example of this is a game of chess or various other board/tile-like games. It'd be great to control how much the computer can make progress in the game with various levels of difficulty for the player. We can also want to let the game decide for us what the next best move is. Something like this is common in three-match type games, such as **Bejeweled**® or **CandyCrush**®, in which you are looking at grid and the game gives you a hint. This type of logic is where **MinMaxAI** comes in.

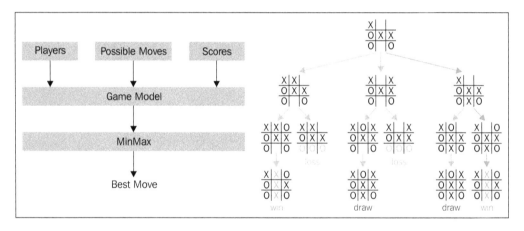

MinMaxAI works by taking an inventory of all of the available moves for our game and placing them into a decision tree. Based on the parameters we give the AI, we can tell it how to choose these decision branches, typically in terms of game difficulty. This is done by taking in the players, a list of all their possible moves as well as their scores, and plugging them into a Game Model protocol that then uses MinMaxAI to determine the best move. The Tic-Tac-Toe example from *WWDC15* is shown in the preceding diagram. Note how some branches would lead to more losses than draws or wins for the computer AI. A harder difficulty level would make the computer *player* choose the paths that more likely lead to a win for it, or, in the case of those three-match games, give the player a suggestion for the next best move.

Of course, as one might have guessed, this type of logic is best for turn-based or tile-based games. MinMaxAI can work in any game, but that game, or at least the implementation of MinMaxAI, will only work if there's a set base of moves and future moves for it to take into its Game Model protocol. An action platformer, unless given some choice of features, wouldn't be able to use MinMaxAI, for example. What's great about this functionality in GameplayKit is that it doesn't need to know the details of your game's rules; it just needs the ability to look into future possible moves.

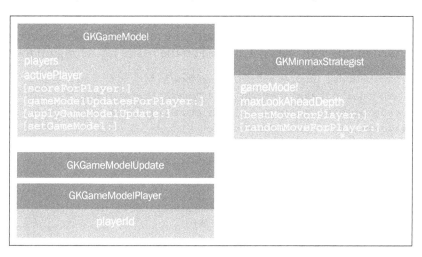

The class diagram shows the classes and functions used when dealing with MinMaxAI. We see GKGameModel, which is actually a protocol for a game state. The GKState objects that adhere to this protocol need to provide a list of players, the active player, the player's score, and the player's list of moves, the latter via the gameModelUpdatesForPlayer() function. We then tell the GKGameModel object what to do as it moves on to the next game move with the applyGameModelUpdate() function. GKGameModelUpdate is essentially an abstract of a game's move and is used by the GKMinMaxStrategist class to build a decision tree, which is thus applied to GKGameModel to change that state in the setGameModel() function.

The GKGameModelPlayer class is a protocol for a player of the game who makes a move, as stated previously, with GKGameModelUpdate. The playerId property is a unique number you can set, which is used to differentiate the players in our game's logic and deal with their own set of moves. This allows the flexibility to have both a hinting structure for the player (or players in a multiplayer game) in addition to also having the computer player have an AI for its own moves. The playerID property is required to adhere to this protocol as we wouldn't know the player we are referencing without it.

The GKMinMaxStrategist class is the actual AI itself that is tied to the gameModel property we created with the prior protocols. The maxLookAheadDepth property is how many moves ahead the AI will look, the more the better and then it returns the best move via the bestMoveForPlayer() function. We can use the randomMoveForPlayer() function to add a bit of randomness to the next move choices; this could be used particularly for the computer's own AI to maybe purposely cause it to make mistakes by choosing a less optimal move.

A quick Objective-C snippet showing how to do this in code is given in the following code. Don't worry about the syntax if you are only familiar with the Swift language we've provided in this book; just get an idea on the basics for setting up these objects.

```
/* ChessGameModel implements GKGameModel */
ChessGameModel *chessGameModel = [ChessGameModel new];
GKMinmaxStrategist *minmax = [GKMinmaxStrategist new];
minmax.gameModel = chessGameModel;
minmax.maxLookAheadDepth = 6;
/* Find the best move for the active player */
ChessGameUpdate *chessGameUpdate =
            [minmax
bestMoveForPlayer:chessGameModel.activePlayer];
/* Apply update to the game model */
[chessGameModel applyGameModelUpdate:chessGameUpdate];
```

This is also, like many of the code snippets in this chapter, taken from the *WWDC15* conference. It uses a chess game as an example. The intricate details of setting up a chess game model are a bit complex, so simply take note of how in this code a ChessGameModel object (which is a child of the abstract GKGameModel class) is first created. Then, we create an object of the GKMinMaxStrategist class named minmax, set its game model, set its maxLookAheadDepth property to 6, and pass the game's move and the current active player to the minMax object. Finally, we update the game's model with the applyGameModelUpdate() function. It's also done in Objective-C at the time of this publication, but check out the FourInaRow demo found here: https://developer.apple.com/library/prerelease/ios/samplecode/FourInARow/Introduction/Intro.html.

This project will let us see a more complete implementation of this AI.

For even more on MinMaxAI, check out the following documentation link:

https://developer.apple.com/library/prerelease/ios/documentation/General/Conceptual/GameplayKit_Guide/Minmax.html.

Next we will talk about adding *controlled* randomness to our games with GameplayKit's random sources.

Random sources

Randomness in games has been a staple of AI, player moves, level design, and game *replayability* since the early days of game development. The rand() function in various programming languages, in addition to a range of numbers to scale that randomness, has typically been used to give our applications some less predictable outcomes. However, games sometimes need to have what we like to call *controlled* randomness. When debugging a game, we don't want to ever run into a problem where a shipped product has an untested state. Sometimes, when using past conventions of randomness, we can run into a situation where the only time some rare events happen may be after a game is out and in the hands of thousands, if not millions, of players who add to the testing pool that we didn't have in the developing phase. Therefore, we may want to control the distribution of randomness. In a typical random selection of outcomes, we get a bell curve of results where the average or middle-ranged outcomes will occur more often than fringe outcomes. This is fine in some games, but rather undesirable in others. Another bit about the rand() function is that its randomness can vary based on other factors, such as the system it's on, the current date and time, and other uncontrollable factors. What we need, then, is platform-independent determinism and customizable distribution. With GameplayKit's random sources, we can accomplish that.

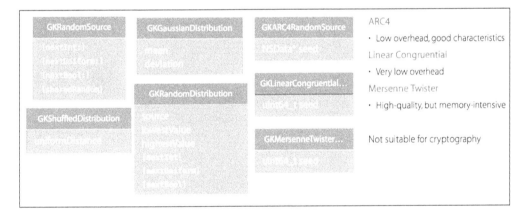

We see a number of the different classes we can use in the preceding image. The base class is GKRandomSource, which actually uses the ARC4 type algorithm by default (via its GKARC4RandomSource subclass). ARC4 is a quick/low overhead and has the typical randomness that we use in many instances. It's different from the arc4Random() C call in which instances of GKARC4RandomSource are independent from each other. GKRandomSource can also become a subclass to either the Linear Congruential or the Mersenne Twister algorithms. Their benefits and disadvantages are shown in the diagram.

It's not recommended that these objects are used for cryptography, so it's best to use other the encryption / hashing frameworks that Apple recommends (https:// developer.apple.com/library/ios/documentation/Security/Conceptual/ cryptoservices/GeneralPurposeCrypto/GeneralPurposeCrypto.html).

The remaining classes give us control of the random number/outcome distribution methodologies. The GKRandDistribution objects let us use helper methods that, for example, give us the ability to create x-sided die pieces in addition to letting us set its lowest and highest range values. The GKGaussianDistribution and GKShuffledDistribution classes also let us use those helper functions, but GKGaussianDistribution is used when we want to have a bell-curve type randomization where the middle values happen more often than the fringe values. Its mean and deviation properties give us controls on that bell curve and if we maybe want more occurrences of fringe values. GKShuffledDistribution, as we can tell from its name, is great for creating an even and complete range distribution, for shuffling decks of cards, or making sure that every value occurs evenly. This class's uniformDistance property is a float between the values of 0.0 and 1.0. At 0.0, all shuffling is completely random; at 1.0, the distribution of all values is even.

Adding random sources to our games is very simple. Here's some code examples using these classes:

```
/* Create a six-sided die with its own random source */
let d6 = GKRandomDistribution.d6()
/* Get die value between 1 and 6 */
let choice = d6.nextInt()
/* Create a custom 256-sided die with its own random source */
let d256 = GKRandomDistribution.die(lowest:1, highest:256)
/* Get die value between 1 and 256 */
let choice = d256.nextInt()
/* Create a twenty-sided die with a bell curve bias */
let d20 = GKGaussianDistribution.d20()
/* Get die value between 1 and 20 that is most likely to
be around 11 */
let choice = d20.nextInt()
/* Create a twenty-sided die with no clustered
values — fair random */
let d20 = GKShuffledDistribution.d20()
/* Get die value between 1 and 20 */
let choice = d20.nextInt()
/* Get another die value that is not the same as
'choice' */
let secondChoice = d20.nextInt()
```

```
/* Make a deck of cards */
var deck = [Ace, King, Queen, Jack, Ten]
/* Shuffle them */
deck = GKRandomSource.sharedRandom().shuffle(deck)
/* possible result - [Jack, King, Ten, Queen, Ace] */
/* Get a random card from the deck */
let card = deck[0]
```

As we can see, these are very quick, simple lines of code that all use the various random source classes. Most are simple property calls, so that when we create our objects in Swift, as seen in the preceding code, it just needs one or two lines of code to utilize these class types and their various randomization functionalities. Combining this to the goal weight of, say, a wander or track AI behavior, and we get some diverse and moderately controlled randomness for the objects and characters in our games.

To read up more on random sources/randomization in this framework, see the documentation link here:

```
https://developer.apple.com/library/prerelease/ios/documentation/
General/Conceptual/GameplayKit_Guide/RandomSources.html
```

Rule systems

Last, but not least, we come to GameplayKit's rule systems. This aspect of the framework uses what's known as **fuzzy logic** or approximations, mainly in the context of transitions between game states. This isn't something all too new to game development. Anyone familiar with linear interpolation will be right at home as this is practically the same concept. Unlike the typical use of linear interpolation, which tends to revolve around transitions between physical actions, GameplayKit's rule systems perform these approximate transitions between various game states. Think of the objects/entities in our games as nouns, the components and actions as verbs, and these rules as the interactions between these verbs and nouns. As we've seen throughout this chapter, this would very much describe game states. So why add an extra layer to this logic? Well, let's look at this example from the GameplayKit announcement. This is where transitions between game states and/or entity-component actions could use this fuzzy logic:

```
if (car.distance < 5) {
  car.slowDown()
}
else if (car.distance >= 5) {
  car.speedUp()
}
```

This pseudo code could represent a car NPC in our game. Maybe a city building game, where there are various car GKAgent objects that have this code as part of their behavior. This seems sound until we get to values at or near 5. What we might notice in our game are a bunch of NPC cars accelerating and braking in a jerky motion. To solve this, we make the transitions between braking and accelerating not be so finite, but instead transition in approximation.

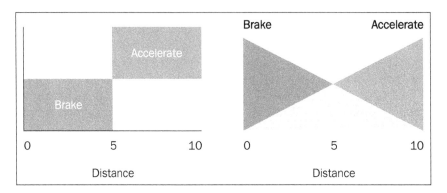

The preceding image is a better illustration of this, with the original logic on the left and fuzzy logic on the right. This creates a smooth transition between actions or states where rule systems come into play; here are the classes we use to implement this type of logic:

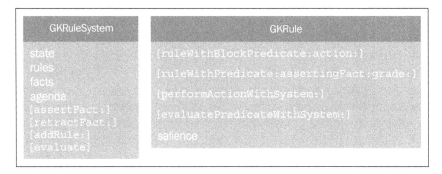

We use the GKRuleSystem and GKRule class instances to utilize rule systems. GKRule represents a specific decision to be made based on an external state, and GKRuleSystem evaluates a set of rules against state data to determine a set of facts. We can assert facts or retract them, and we can grade the *fuzziness* factor between these rules.

Let's take a look at this in code to get a better feel for it:

```
/* Make a rule system */
GKRuleSystem* sys = [[GKRuleSystem alloc] init];
/* Getting distance and asserting facts */
float distance = sys.state[@"distance"];
[sys assertFact:@"close" grade:1.0f - distance /
kBrakingDistance];
[sys assertFact:@"far" grade:distance / kBrakingDistance];
/* Grade our facts - farness and closeness */
float farness = [sys gradeForFact@"far"];
float closeness = [sys gradeForFact@"close"];
/* Derive Fuzzy acceleration */
float fuzzyAcceleration = farness - closeness;
[car applyAcceleration:fuzzyAcceleration withDeltaTime:seconds];
```

First, the sys object of GKRuleSystem is created, and we grab the distance state value and save that to the distance variable. We then assert/add a rule named close that happens if 1.0f - distance / kBrakingDistance. The next finite rule we add is far, which is defined as distance / kBrakingDistance, or basically any distance greater than 1 - distance / kBrakingDistance. We create new fuzzy values of close and far, named farness and closeness, that are based on the gradeForFact property of GKRuleSystem. Then, from this, we get our fuzzyAcceleration value from the difference between farness and closeness and apply that acceleration to our car. This is checked during the update render cycle automatically and keeps the logic transitions smooth, removing jerky movements between the different states.

This simple example code from *WWDC15* is in Objective-C, but we can see more examples (some in Swift) in the full documentation page as follows:

```
https://developer.apple.com/library/prerelease/ios/documentation/
General/Conceptual/GameplayKit_Guide/RuleSystems.html
```

We can also see some of this implemented in the demo projects we linked to previously.

With these classes, we can create a number of complex rule systems that transition in a more fluid fashion.

Summary

This chapter has gone into a great deal of this deep and independent game-centric framework. We have first reviewed the basic concepts of entities and components, and how GameplayKit takes advantage of the component-based structuring. We then moved on to a staple of game development, the concept of state machines, and how GameplayKit utilizes them. Then, we have reviewed ways by which we can automatically control components and entities in our games with agents, goals, and behaviors, as well as Pathfinding's navigation graphs that add to this automation. We have learned that MinMaxAI lets us hint future moves to the player or give the computer a smart way of challenging us in various turn-based games. Finally, we have seen how random sources add controllable variety to outcomes in our games, whereas Rule systems can keep transitions of various states from being too finite. There's much more to GameplayKit than we could show here, so it's highly recommended that you read through some of the documentation links provided earlier to get an even better feel for what this framework has to offer. In the next chapter, we move on to the Metal API as well as some other tricks and tips that aid best in making the most out of your game and keeping your games at that all too crucial 60 fps.

6
Exhibit the Metal in Your Game

Up to this point, we have learned quite a bit. We looked into Apple's Swift programming language, got an idea of the general flow of an iOS app, and how to control that through code and/or storyboards. We got an understanding of how 2D games and 2D overlays can be made with **SpriteKit** and how 3D games can be designed even in the **Xcode** editor with SceneKit. Finally, we reviewed how to create reusable game logic, components, and AI with the various aspects of **GameplayKit**.

Essentially, this is all that is needed to get right to planning, coding, and building your own games. If there's a game idea that has come to your mind at this time, go right ahead and start planning it out. The frameworks and Xcode features from the past chapters can help take your abstract ideas and start turning them into what could soon be a playable application.

However, before moving forward, we'd like to take this time to go over a few more tips, tricks, and topics that we either briefly mentioned or have yet to go over. These topics mainly cover the ways we can optimize our games and get more out of the Apple hardware. In this chapter, we shall review a bit on the rather advanced topic of the Apple Metal low-level graphics API.

Just a warning that the topic of low-level graphics APIs can get rather advanced. This won't be an all-encompassing tutorial on the subject; more of an upper-level summary and a way to appreciate all that SpriteKit and SceneKit do in the background for us. We hope that, at the very least, it makes you wish to pursue how to build your own custom rendering objects that might potentially allow the development of extremely performant and detailed games.

The Apple Metal API and the graphics pipeline

One of the rules, if not *the golden rule* of modern video game development, is to keep our games running constantly at 60 frames per second or greater. If developing for VR devices and applications, this is of even more importance as dropped frame rates could lead to a sickening and game ending experience for the player.

In the past, being lean was the name of the game; hardware limitations prevented much from not only being written to the screen but how much memory storage a game could hold. This limited the number of scenes, characters, effects, and levels. In the past, game development was built more with an engineering mindset, so the developers made the things work with what little they had. Many of the games on 8-bit systems and earlier had levels and characters that were only different because of elaborate sprite slicing and recoloring.

Over time, advances in hardware, particularly that of GPUs allowed for richer graphical experiences. This leads to the advent of computation-heavy 3D models, real-time lighting, robust shaders, and other effects that we can use to make our games present an even greater player experience; this while trying to stuff it all in that precious .016666 second/60 Hz window.

To get everything out of the hardware and combat the clash between a designer's need to make the best looking experience and the engineering reality of hardware limitations in even today's CPU/GPUs, Apple developed the Metal API.

CPU/GPU framework levels

Metal is what's known as a low-level GPU API. When we build our games on the iOS platform, there are different levels between the machine code in our GPU/CPU hardware and what we use to design our games. This goes for any piece of computer hardware we work with, be it Apple or others. For example, on the CPU side of things, at the very base of it all is the **machine code**. The next level up is the **assembly language** of the chipset. Assembly language differs based on the CPU chipset and allows the programmer to be as detailed as determining the individual registers to swap data in and out of in the processor. Just a few lines of a for-loop in C/C++ would take up a decent number of lines to code in assembly. The benefit of working in the lower levels of code is that we could make our games run much faster. However, most of the mid-upper level languages/APIs are made to work well enough so that this isn't a necessity anymore.

Game developers have coded in assembly even after the very early days of game development. In the late 1990's, the game developer Chris Sawyer created his game, **Rollercoster Tycoon™**, almost entirely in the x86 assembly language! Assembly can be a great challenge for any enthusiastic developer who loves to tinker with the inner workings of computer hardware.

Moving up the chain we have where C/C++ code would be and just above that is where we'd find Swift and Objective-C code. Languages such as Ruby and JavaScript, which some developers can use in Xcode, are yet another level up.

That was about the CPU, now on to the GPU. The **Graphics Processing Unit (GPU)** is the coprocessor that works with the CPU to make the calculations for the visuals we see on the screen. The following diagram shows the GPU, the APIs that work with the GPU, and possible iOS games that can be made based on which framework/API is chosen.

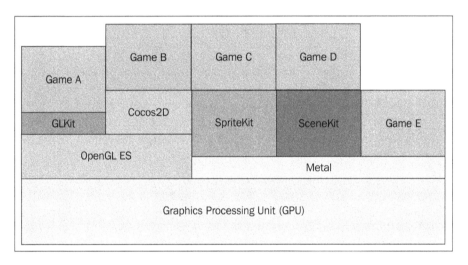

Like the CPU, the lowest level is the processor's machine code. To work as close to the GPU's machine code as possible, many developers would use Silicon Graphics' **OpenGL API**. For mobile devices, such as the iPhone and iPad, it would be the OpenGL subset, **OpenGL ES**. Apple provides a helper framework/library to OpenGL ES named **GLKit**. GLKit helps simplify some of the shader logic and lessen the manual work that goes into working with the GPU at this level. For many game developers, this was practically the only option to make 3D games on the iOS device family originally; though some use of iOS's Core Graphics, Core Animation and UIKit frameworks were perfectly fine for simpler games.

Not too long into the lifespan of the iOS device family, third-party frameworks came into play, which were aimed at game development. Using OpenGL ES as its base, thus sitting directly one level above it, is the **Cocos2D framework**. This was actually the framework used in the original release of Rovio's Angry Birds™ series of games back in 2009. Eventually, Apple realized how important gaming was for the success of the platform and made their own game-centric frameworks, that is, the SpriteKit and SceneKit frameworks. They too, like Cocos2D/3D, sat directly above OpenGL ES. When we made SKSprite nodes or SCNNodes in our Xcode projects, up until the introduction of Metal, OpenGL operations were being used to draw these objects in the update/render cycle behind the scenes. As of iOS 9, SpriteKit and SceneKit use Metal's rendering pipeline to process graphics to the screen. If the device is older, they revert to OpenGL ES as the underlying graphics API.

Graphics pipeline overview

This topic can be a book all on its own, but let's take a look at the graphics pipeline to get an idea, at least on an upper level, of what the GPU is doing during a single rendered frame. We can imagine the graphical data of our games being divided in two main categories:

- **Vertex data**: This is the position information of where on the screen this data can be rendered. Vector/vertex data can be expressed as points, lines, or triangles. Remember the old saying about video game graphics, "everything is a triangle." All of those polygons in a game are just a collection of triangles via their point/vector positions. The GPU's **Vertex Processing Unit** (**VPU**) handles this data.

- **Rendering/pixel data**: Controlled by the GPU's Rasterizer, this is the data that tells the GPU how the objects, positioned by the vertex data, will be colored/shaded on the screen. For example, this is where color channels, such as RGB and alpha, are handled. In short, it's the pixel data and what we actually see on the screen.

Here's a diagram showing the graphics pipeline overview:

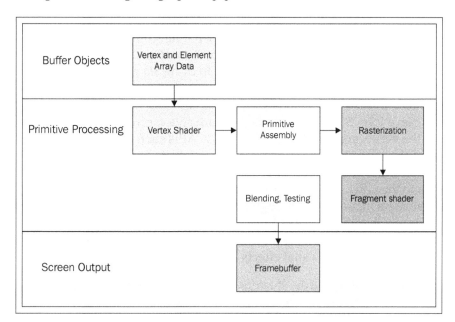

The graphics pipeline is the sequence of steps it takes to have our data rendered to the screen. The previous diagram is a simplified example of this process. Here are the main sections that can make up the pipeline:

- **Buffer objects**: These are known as **Vertex Buffer Objects** in OpenGL and are of the class `MTLBuffer` in the Metal API. These are the objects we create in our code that are sent from the CPU to the GPU for **primitive processing**. These objects contain data, such as the positions, normal vectors, alphas, colors, and more.

- **Primitive processing**: These are the steps in the GPU that take our Buffer Objects, break down the various vertex and rendering data in those objects, and then draw this information to the frame buffer, which is the screen output we see on the device.

Before we go over the steps of primitive processing done in Metal, we should first understand the history and basics of shaders.

What are shaders?

GPUs first came into use because of none other than the video game industry. Arcade cabinets in the 1970's had GPU chips separate from the main CPU to handle the specialized visual needs of the games compared with other computing applications at the time. Eventually, the need to draw 3D graphics in games in the mid-1990's led to the modern GPU architecture we have now. Shaders were actually first introduced in 1988 by Pixar back when the company was run by Apple's cofounder Steve Jobs. Shaders are little programs we can write directly to the GPU to process the vertex and pixel data. Originally, APIs such as OpenGL ES 1.0 didn't make use of shader processing but instead were what's known as fixed-function APIs. In fixed-function APIs, programmers just referenced simple set rendering commands to the GPU. As GPUs evolved and took more work away from the CPU, the use of shaders increased. Although a rather more advanced way to traverse the graphics pipeline than the fixed-function methodology, shaders allow for even deeper customization of what the GPU displays to the screen. Game developers and 3D artists continue to push visual effects in games with them.

From OpenGL 2.0 and onwards, shaders were built in the API's C-like language named GLSL. In the Apple Metal API, we build shaders with the Metal Shading Language, which is a subset of C++11 of the file type `.metal` and can run the pipeline in either Objective-C or Swift with our view controllers.

Types of shaders

Shaders come in a number of types that continue to grow as 3D games and art animation continues to progress. The most commonly used are Vertex shaders and Fragment shaders. Vertex shaders are used to transform 3D coordinates into 2D coordinates for the screen to display, in short, the positioning data of our graphics. Fragment shaders, also known as Pixel shaders, are what are used to convert colors and other visual attributes of pixels on the screen. These other attributes of Fragment Shaders can include bump mapping, shadows, and specific highlights as well. We emphasized the word *attributes* because that's usually the name given for the properties or input of our shader programs.

Here is a code sample of a simple Vertex and Fragment shader written in the Metal Shading Language.

```
//Shaders.metal
// (1)
#include <metal_stdlib>
using namespace metal;
// (2)
```

```
vertex float4 basic_vertex(
//(3)
  const device packed_float3* vertex_array [[ buffer(0) ]],
//(4)
  unsigned int vertexID [[ vertex_id ]]) {
//(5)
  return float4(vertex_array[vertexID], 1.0);
}
//(6)
fragment half4 basic_fragment() {
  return half4(1.0);
```

The code here is a bit different than what we've seen throughout the course of the book. Let's go over it line by line.

1. The Metal Shading Language is a C++11-like language, so we see that the Metal Standard Library is imported into the shader file with the line `#include <metal_stdlib>` in addition to `using namespace metal;`

2. The next line is the creation of our Vertex shader using the keyword `vertex`. This shader is a vertex of four floats. Why four floats when 3D space only deals with *x*, *y*, and *z* coordinates? To summarize, 3D matrix math involves a fourth component, *w*, to accurately handle the math calculations of 3D space. In short if *w*= *0*, the *x*, *y*, and *z* coordinates are vectors; if *w* = *1*, then those coordinates are points. The purpose of this shader will be to draw simple points to the screen, so *w* will be 1.0.

3. Here, we create a pointer to an array of float3 type (holders for our *x*, *y*, and *z* coordinates) and set it to the very first buffer with the `[[ buffer(0) ]]` declaration. The `[[ ]]` syntax is used to declare inputs/attributes for our shaders.

4. The unsigned integer `vertexID` is what we name the `vertex_id` attribute of this particular array of vertices.

5. This is where the float4 type is returned, or in this case, the final position of this vertex array. We see that it returns two sections of the output: the first being the reference to this vertex array, identified by the `vertex_id` attribute and the `w` value of `1.0`, to represent that these are points in space.

6. This line is where we create the fragment shader, using the `fragment` keyword. This shader is of the data type `half4`, which is an array of [4,4] 16-bit floats. This is, in this case, ultimately to create 16-bit colored pixels. The data in this [4,4]-component vector type saves 16 bits to R, G, B, and alpha channels. This shader is going to simply show pure white pixel shading with no transparency, so we simply write `return half4(1.0);`. This sets all of the bits to 1, which is equivalent to `rgba(1,1,1,1)`.

When we create a Buffer Object, which can just be a Struct of floating points on the screen, we pass that data through these shaders and out would pop up a white triangle or set of triangle shapes on the screen.

Looking back at the *Graphics pipeline* diagram, we see that after the vertex shader is calculated, the GPU does what's known as **Primitive Assembly**. This is essentially where the points and vectors defined in the vertex shader are mapped to coordinates in screen space. The Rasterizer step, in simple terms, then figures from the vertex data where and how we can and can't color that pixel data onto the screen using the fragment shader information. After taking in the fragment shader information, the GPU then uses that information for the blending of that pixel data. Finally, that output is sent to or committed to the frame buffer where the player sees that output. This all happens in a single draw call in the render cycle. Having all of your game's lights, pixels, effects, physics, and other graphics cycle through this in .016666 seconds is the name of the game.

We'll go over some more Metal code later but understand for now that shaders are like little instruction factories for data input we send to them in our Swift/Object-C code. Other shader types that have arisen over the years are Geometry Shaders and Tessellation Shaders.

 Both the Vertex and Fragment shaders are present in this single `.metal` file, but typically shaders are written in separate files. Xcode and Metal will combine all `.metal` files in your project, so it doesn't matter if the shaders are in one file or not. OpenGL's GLSL for the most part forces the separation of shader types.

For years, OpenGL worked well for many different GPUs but as we all see, Apple Metal allows us to perform draw calls up to 10x times faster than OpenGL ES.

Why is Metal faster than OpenGL ES?

In late 2013, Apple announced the **iPhone 5s**. Built into the 5s was the **A7 Processor**, the first 64 bit GPU for the iOS device family. It provided a decent graphical boost compared with prior devices and reflected how GPUs in mobile devices were quickly catching up to gaming consoles released just a few years prior. OpenGL, though a staple in low-level graphics APIs, didn't squeeze the most out of the A7 chip.

Seen in the next diagram, the interaction between the CPU and GPU doesn't always perform the optimal way we'd want it to for our games.

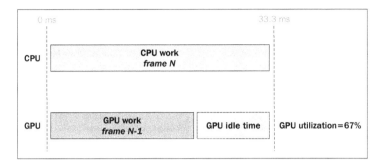

Be it textures, shaders, or render targets, draw calls use their own state vector. The CPU via the low-level API uses much of that time verifying the state of the draw call. This process is very expensive for the CPU. What happens is that in many cycles, the GPU is sitting idle, waiting for the CPU to finish its past instruction. Here's what's taking up all of that time in the API:

- **State validation**: Confirming API usage is valid. This encodes API state to the hardware state.

- **Shader compilation**: Runtime generation of the shader machine code. This deals with interactions between the state and shaders.

- **Sending work to the GPU**: Managing resource residency batching commands.

What Apple did with their Metal API is do these steps in a smarter fashion. Shader compilation is done during the application's load time. There's no need to reload the shaders every cycle; this was simply a relic of older hardware limitations. This is why in our previous code example, we can build more than one shader in one Metal file, while this was prohibited in OpenGL ES. State validation, though important, doesn't need to be checked every cycle. Checking the state validation can be set to happen only when new content is loaded.

Even with Metal's advantages, this is why it's recommended to store 2D animations in **SpriteSheets**. We mentioned SpriteSheets back in our discussion of on SpritKit. They are a collection of sprites fitted onto one texture. The graphics pipeline then only has to deal with one version of that content. Internally under the hood of SpriteKit, the GPU then doesn't have to do as many state vector calls compared to having each character animation being placed on its own separate texture.

The last process for the CPU is when it sends the information out to the GPU for processing. This is going to be done during each draw call, and in either Metal or Open GL ES, it will still be this process that will happen the most frequently. Here is the result of this internal, low-level restructuring done in the Metal API:

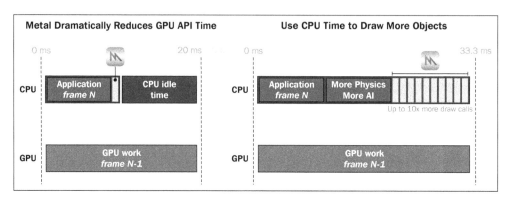

As we see in the diagram from *WWDC14*, there are up to 10 extra draw calls that can be added during the render cycle! We can use that time saved for other processes instead of extra draw calls, such as more physics or AI in our games.

The cycle diagrams shown are from the original Metal API announcement at *WWDC2014* and used a frame rate of 30 fps. If developing for VR where 60 fps or greater is necessary for a working game, these numbers are halved. Either way this is rather impressive for mobile device GPUs. Search online for games made in Metal and you'd be impressed. With this much room to add more to our game during each render cycle, there's no reason not to have an impressive game at the full 60 fps. Additionally, as of iOS 9, the SpriteKit and SceneKit frameworks by default are backed by Metal. Even if the Metal API is too much to understand, we can still utilize these render saving benefits from what we already learned about these frameworks.

The basic Metal object/code structure

To finish off our talk about Apple Metal, let's look at an overview of the API's object and code structuring. We already briefly saw some shader code in the Metal Shading Language, so let's see how we can work with this API in our projects.

Objects	Purpose
Device	Reference to the GPU
Command queue	Serial sequence of command buffers
Command buffer	Contains GPU hardware commands
Command encoder	Translates API commands to GPU hardware commands
State	Framebuffer configuration, depth, samplers, blend, and so on
Code	Shaders (vertex, fragment, geometry, and tessellation)
Resources	Textures and Data Buffer Objects (vertices, constants, and so on)

The preceding table represents the various types of objects that we'd work with if writing a game directly in the Metal API. They are the Device, the State, the Command Buffer, our Shaders, Textures, and many more.

We can import the Metal API into `ViewController.swift` class with the following:

```
import Metal
import QuartzCore
```

This imports the Metal API. The QuartzCore API is needed as well since the `CAMetalLayer` object we will work with is a member of that library. Also, make sure that you set your target device to an actual iOS device as new or newer than the iPhone 5S, the Xcode simulator does not support Metal. Otherwise, Xcode will give you the *Could Not Build* Objective-C model `Metal` error. This is true as of the writing of this book with the Xcode 7 Beta. Over time and probably after the official public release of the El Capitan OS, this will no longer be needed. For now, to test your own custom Metal code, you will have to test on an actual device. Doing so will involve having to pay for your own Apple Development account. More on this is given in the next chapter.

Here's the order in which we'd have to work with the objects in the table shown previously as well as some code samples in Swift that accomplish these steps:

1. Create the reference to the Device with the `MTLDevice` class as:

```
let device: MTLDevice = MTLCreateSystemDefaultDevice()
```

2. Create a `CAMetalLayer` object for these objects to be placed on the screen as:

```
let metalLayer = CAMetalLayer()
```

3. Create Vertex Data/Buffer Object(s) (VBOs) to send data to shaders as follows:

```
/*Simple Vertex Data object, an array of floats that draws a
simple triangle to the screen */
let vertexData:[Float] = [
    0.0, 1.0, 0.0,
   -1.0, -1.0, 0.0,
    1.0, -1.0, 0.0]
```

4. Create our shaders that will work with these VBOs.

   We did this in our previous shader code samples. The vertex data combined with our previously made shaders together create a simple white triangle to the screen.

5. Set up a Render Pipeline as follows:

```
//Library objects that reference our shaders we created
let library = device.newDefaultLibrary()!
//constant where we pass the vertex shader function
let vertexFunction =
library.newFunctionWithName("basic_vertex")
//now the fragment shader
let fragmentFunction =
library.newFunctionWithName("basic_fragment")

/*Describes the Render Pipeline and sets the vertex and
fragment shaders of the Render Pipeine*/
let pipelineStateDescriptor = MTLRenderPipelineDescriptor()
//initiates the descriptor's vertex and fragment shader
function properties with the constants we created prior
pipelineStateDescriptor.vertexFunction = vertexFunction
pipelineStateDescriptor.fragmentFunction = fragmentFunction

//Makes the pixel format an 8bit color format
pipelineStateDescriptor.colorAttachments.
objectAtIndexedSubscript(0).
```

```
pixelFormat = .BGRA8Unorm

/*Checks if we described the Render Pipeline correctly,
otherwise, throws an error. */
var pipelineError : NSError?
pipelineState = device.
newRenderPipelineStateWithDescriptor(
pipelineStateDescriptor, error: &pipelineError)
if pipelineState == nil {
  println("Pipeline state not created, error
\(pipelineError)")
```

6. Create a command queue as follows:

```
var commandQueue = device.newCommandQueue()
```

To actually render these objects in our game, we'd have to do the following processes in our view controller:

1. Create a display link. This is a timer that refreshes every time the screen refreshes. It's a member of the class `CADisplayLink` and at every screen refresh, we call the `gameRenderLoop` function.

   ```
   var timer = CADisplayLink(target: self, selector:
   Selector("gameRenderLoop"))
   timer.addToRunLoop(NSRunLoop.mainRunLoop(), forMode:
   NSDefaultRunLoopMode)
   ```

   The `gameRenderLoop` function can look like the following. It calls the soon-to-be filled in function, `render()`:

   ```
   func gameRenderloop() {
     autoreleasepool {
       self.render()
     }
   ```

2. Create a Render Pass Descriptor. For this example, a mostly red texture is to be created around our white triangle as shown here:

   ```
   let passDescriptor = MTLRenderPassDescriptor()
   passDescriptor.colorAttachments[0].texture =
   drawable.texture
   passDescriptor.colorAttachments[0].loadAction = .Clear
   passDescriptor.colorAttachments[0].storeAction = .Store
   passDescriptor.colorAttachments[0].clearColor =
   MTLClearColorMake(0.8, 0.0, 0.0, 1.0)
   ```

3. Create a Command Buffer in our `render()` function:

```
let commandBuffer = commandQueue.commandBuffer()
```

4. Create a Render Command Encoder. In other words, a set of commands for `commandQueue`. In the code example given later, this tells the GPU to draw triangles with the VBO we created earlier. This is placed (in this example) in the `render()` function.

```
let renderEncoderOpt = commandBuffer.
renderCommandEncoderWithDescriptor(renderPassDescriptor)
if let renderEncoder = renderEncoderOpt {
  renderEncoder.setRenderPipelineState(pipelineState)
  renderEncoder.setVertexBuffer(vertexBuffer,
  offset: 0, atIndex: 0)
  renderEncoder.drawPrimitives(.Triangle,
  vertexStart: 0, vertexCount: 3, instanceCount: 1)
  renderEncoder.endEncoding()
}
```

5. Commit your Command Buffer. This essentially tells the GPU to do its draw call based on the commands that have been packed into the `commandBuffer` object. Place this after the past code's `if` statement in the `render()` function.

```
commandBuffer.presentDrawable(drawable)
commandBuffer.commit()
```

That is the short of it. That's the general process of drawing a simple triangle to the screen and manually creating the render loop on the GPU.

Should you rather opt for SpriteKit and SceneKit to do all of this manual work for you? That would be understandable. Remember though, like when playing a game on hard mode, it comes with its rewards to take the harder route. Yes, as of iOS 9, the SpriteKit and SceneKit frameworks are default to Metal. Game engines, such as Unity and Unreal Engine, even implement Metal when converting projects to the platform. However, knowing how to build your games in a low-level graphics API, such as Metal or OpenGL, will give the developer the ability to have the potential for most lean/fast performing game for the device family. Be sure to check out some of the games created with Metal next time you search online. They can really give your players a great experience. At the same time, this can challenge your skills as a game developer since being a game developer is the combination of an artist, engineer, and computer scientist. Working directly in the GPU's basic functions will challenge all of that.

To dive more into the rabbit hole that is low-level graphics development with Metal, check out these links:

- `https://developer.apple.com/metal/`
- `https://developer.apple.com/library/ios/documentation/Metal/Reference/MetalShadingLanguageGuide/data-types/data-types.html`
- `http://www.raywenderlich.com/77488/ios-8-metal-tutorial-swift-getting-started`
- `https://realm.io/news/3d-graphics-metal-swift/`

The first link is to the official Apple Developer page for Metal. The next link is Apple's list of data types used in the Metal API. The last two links are two separate tutorials to make simple Metal scenes in Swift. Some of the code we used can be found in these tutorials as well as full Xcode projects. The first of these two links are to the iOS tutorial site `www.raywenderlich.com`. The last link is to a page that has a great video presentation and full instructions on Swift and Metal 3D graphics by former Apple Engineer, *Warren Moore*.

Summary

Congrats on getting this far. If this book were a game, we'd probably have earned an achievement for this chapter alone. As we saw, working with a low-level API such as Metal can be a bit daunting. We first reviewed what it means when developers and engineers mention lower and upper level frameworks and code. On the CPU side, we saw that the lowest level is the machine's code with Swift and Objective-C in the middle, and above C/C++ and Assembly code. Next, we spoke about the GPU side and where the visual graphics APIs we've gone over in the past chapters stand in the hierarchy. We then got an understanding of the history of lower-level graphics APIs such as OpenGL ES, how the graphic pipeline generally works under the hood, and how to make basic shaders. Finally, we reviewed why Metal is faster during the render cycle than OpenGL, the general structure behind Metal, and some of the code/objects used to manually set up the render loop. This chapter merely scratched the surface on this topic, so if you are up to the challenge, it's highly recommended to continue reading documentation on how Metal can make your games stand out from the rest.

At this point, you should now have all that it takes to make a game on the iOS platform. The last essential lesson for iOS game development is learning how to test, publish, and update your published game in the app store. In the next chapter, let's learn how to get that game on the Apple app store.

7
Publishing Our iOS Game

Creating a great game is hard work. Our goal as game developers is to have an application that can be played by thousands, if not millions of people. We want them to play what we crafted in those long weeks and months. Before the app is released, we'd also probably want to have others test the game to weed out any bugs that might have been missed. Publishing on the iOS platform can allow us to do both.

We can allow others to try out our games before release through the **TestFlight** service, and of course, we can then submit our game for release on the Apple App Store. After release, we can submit updates. These updates and future versions could be just to patch up some minor bugs we might have missed in the initial releases, add new features, such as levels, achievements, and other Apple services, or we might need to update our app later on to adhere to the eventual updates that will happen with the iOS platform.

In this chapter, we are going to cover a few main topics:

- Setting up our apps for either testing or publishing in iTunes Connect
- Steps to submit our app to be played in the app store
- Summary of the TestFlight service for testing in the prerelease phase
- How to use iTunes Connect to create updates to our app

We won't tell you how to market your game, as that's an entire book/topic on its own that depends on your budget and preferences. However, we will say that if you or your beta testers found playing your game fun, there is a chance that others will too. Submitting to the app store does not warrant instant success.

Even unreleased games that get high accolades at the ever growing list of indie game reward shows or game jams might not have seen that praise reflected in sales and downloads after release. We have to remember that the game development scene, thanks in part to gaming's position in popular culture, is a sea of thousands of developers, both big and small, trying to make the next great game.

Don't let that discourage you though. If your game does well, which it has the ability to with the Apple App Store, then it could be a life-changing experience. No matter the outcome, let the experience of building your own game and learning this development platform humble you and make you want to be an even better developer for your next project. Eventually, that hard work will pay off.

The ever changing process of app submission

Before we move forward in explaining the steps needed to publish your game, we wanted to note a little fact about this subject. This fact is that the exact steps needed to submit our iOS apps for testing or publication is one that changes rather often. Every couple of months this process might change from how we describe it here.

Over the years, since the start of iOS development, Apple has continually made this process easier and more streamlined. Xcode does much more of the signing/provisioning work for us than it did in the past, and the worries of our app taking forever to appear in the App Store are hardly an issue.

For example, when the Swift game PikiPop was submitted in November, 2014, it only took five business days between the day it was submitted for review to when it appeared in the App Store for the public. This review time will vary for each of us, but as long as there aren't any terrible errors or policy violations in our apps, we can expect our creations to be public for millions to potentially play. To make sure that the publication of your game goes smoothly, it's best to review the App Review Guidelines found here: `https://developer.apple.com/app-store/review/guidelines/`.

> We wrote this book in the late summer of 2015, so if you are reading this at a much later date and feel some of these processes might be out of date, make sure to see the most recent updates here on Apple's own App submission documentation page:
>
> `https://developer.apple.com/library/ios/documentation/LanguagesUtilities/Conceptual/iTunesConnect_Guide/Chapters/SubmittingTheApp.html`

Before submitting your app

There is one more potential development snag we must warn about before you choose to submit your app to the app store. As of the time of this publication, if you build your app in a beta version of Xcode, that app will be rejected from review.

During the course of this book, we have been building our apps and going over features that currently are in the beta version of Xcode 7. This was because there are a number of new features for iOS 9 / Xcode 7 that weren't there in iOS 8 / Xcode 6, namely, the GameplayKit framework and visual editor tools for SceneKit that make Xcode development as hands on as multiplatform game engines.

By the time you are reading this, Xcode 7 should no longer be in the beta phase. Therefore, you should be able to publish an iOS 9 (or later) game without worrying if these features are *beta only*.

When you build your games for releasing to the App Store, make sure to first build them in the current non-beta version of Xcode. Use the beta versions of Xcode to test the newest unreleased features as well as up and coming iOS builds during the prerelease phase.

Preparing our apps for iTunes Connect

So you have coded, simulated, and hopefully enjoyed playing a bit of that iOS game you worked so much on. The next step is to bring your app into the beta/prerelease phase. The goal of this phase is to get your game into the hands of a smaller pool of gamers/testers to simulate what the experience could be for the thousands, if not millions of people who could potentially play your game. The very first step to this, if you haven't already, is to sign up for the Apple Developer Program: `https://developer.apple.com/programs/`.

There is a cost involved and that cost will be based on your development goals. For individual, sole proprietor business accounts, it costs $99 a year to be an iOS developer. If you are working as part of a group of developers, then the Enterprise plan of $299.99 might be a better choice.

In your developer page, you will also have to make sure that your provisioning profile is set up correctly. This step used to be one of the toughest things to complete in being an iOS developer, but Xcode has made this process more automated with each new update. If you've been testing your app in Xcode with an actual device, you've obviously already done this step. If not, here's more information on setting up your provision profile(s): `https://developer.apple.com/library/mac/documentation/NetworkingInternet/Conceptual/RemoteNotificationsPG/Chapters/ProvisioningDevelopment.html`.

The portal that will be your best friend in the process of publishing your app is iTunes Connect here:

`https://itunesconnect.apple.com/`

iTunes Connect is where you can see your submitted apps, track various app analytics, assign TestFlight beta testers, and view your app's revenue. We won't be able to give a full rundown of every feature available in iTunes Connect; mainly we'll look at the steps needed to post, publish, and update your game. Feel free to dive into all of the features and settings that iTunes Connect can provide for your app as the features grow with every new iOS update.

Submitting your app in the testing/beta phase

Let's get right into the steps needed to submit your app. First, we shall talk about the testing/beta phase of your game.

Here is a summary of the steps needed for the testing/beta phase of your game:

1. Create an iTunes Connect app record.
2. Update the build string.
3. Archive and validate your app.
4. Upload your app to iTunes Connect.
5. Beta test your game with the TestFlight service.
6. Analyze crash reports and solicit feedback from testers.

Steps *1-4* are the same for both the testing and release phase of your game.

Creating an iTunes Connect app record

These are the steps needed to add your App to the iTunes Connect app record:

1. Log into your account at `https://itunesconnect.apple.com/` and go to the **My Apps** section.

2. Now click on the **+** icon located on the top-left corner of the page and pick **New iOS App** from the dropdown.

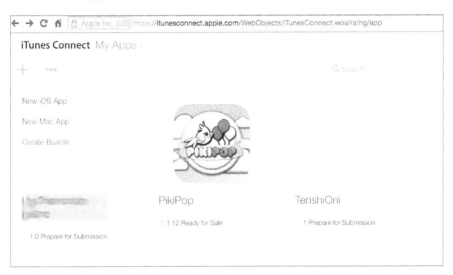

3. Fill in the appropriate fields and click on **Create** if you already know the information for this data. For those unsure what to place here, we review each of these fields in the following screenshot:

Note the **SKU**, the **Version**, and the **Bundle ID** fields. The SKU must be unique and not in use already as Apple will use this for the identification of your app in the store. The **Version** and **Bundle ID** fields must match the build settings you have set in your game's Xcode project. The **Bundle ID** field is a dropdown that at first might only show the Wildcard App/Bundle ID.

The Wildcard ID is one of two types of Bundle IDs, the other being the Explicit App ID. Here's a link to Apple's documentation/FAQ for which type of ID would be best for your game: `https://developer.apple.com/library/ios/qa/qa1713/_index.html`. In short, if you are going to use Apple services, such as Notifications and Game Center achievements, you would need an Explicit App ID, if not, then the Wildcard ID is best.

 If you wish to use the Explicit Bundle ID, you will have to register your app's Bundle ID in the Apple Developer portal. The IDs that are registered on the Developer portal will populate that dropdown. Here's the link to that page in the developer site: `https://developer.apple.com/account/ios/identifiers/bundle/bundleCreate.action`.

The **Bundle ID Suffix** field is found in your project's `info.plist` file. It's a unique string that is created by your Xcode project, also known as the Bundle Seed ID. We'll show you where to find this and other bundle/build-based information when we go over the *Updating the build string* step next.

The **Name** field is what your game's name will be in the App Store. This is what people searching for and hopefully visiting your game's landing page will see. The **Primary Language** dropdown is what your game's default language will be if the app store can't localize your game's information for that territory.

Updating the build string

The build string represents an iteration of your game's bundle. It's a two-period-separated list of positive integers, as in *1.2.3*. Basically, the build string is another layer of versioning added for your game. When making an iOS app, as in our case, changing this build information will automatically be seen by iTunes Connect during the upload step. If we don't update this field, even if we change our game's code, iTunes connect will still think that you are trying to upload the same build and will reject your upload.

Here's where you can find this information in your Xcode project:

The bundle identifier, build string, version number, and other app identification/ global settings are found on the **General** tab in the Inspector window when we click on the project's main file in the Navigation pane. We can also find this information represented in the `info.plist` file. Make sure that these fields match your iTunes Connect record.

Now let's move on to uploading our game in Xcode to iTunes Connect.

Archive and validate your app

The next step in the app publishing process is to archive your game's project bundle. To do this, go to the top dropdown menus and then navigate to **Project | Archive**. The archive selection might be inaccessible if your test device is the simulator as to the iOS Device.

Once built, your archived app will be seen in the Archives organizer with other archives you have created from this and other apps. This window will open when you build the archive, but it can be accessed at any time by going to **Window | Organizer** in the top menu.

The window can be seen in the following screenshot:

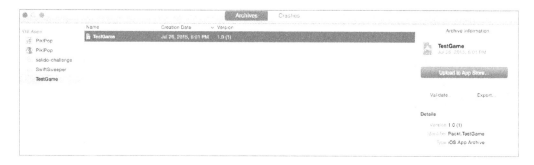

Next, we validate your game to make sure that it fits the minimum requirements for submission. To do this, follow these steps:

1. Click on the **Validate** button found on the right side of the preceding Archives organizer window.

2. A pop-up window will show where you choose the Development Team that would do the provisioning for this app. (This is assuming your Provisioning profile was set up correctly.) Click on **Choose** to move to the next step.

3. This will open more of the popup showing a summary of your app before performing the actual validation. Information such as your app's Bundle ID along with the Bundle Seed ID mentioned earlier can be seen here as well.

4. Click on **Validate** and if the information in your app project is correctly matching what we set up on iTunes Connect, then your app should be validated and ready for submission to iTunes Connect and eventually the App Store itself.

If your app is not validated, make sure that all of your information in iTunes Connect matches, most importantly the Bundle ID.

The *App validation* step could probably be skipped just by clicking on the **Upload To App Store...** button, but is a good way to test early on if everything check out with our game.

More on app validation can be found here:

```
https://developer.apple.com/library/mac/recipes/xcode_help-archives_
organizer/articles/ValidatingYourApp.html
```

Upload your app to iTunes Connect

This step should now be rather simple. Click on the blue **Upload To App Store...** button, and you should get the same prompts seen from the app validation stage. You'll be asked to choose the Development Team; show your app's details, and you can choose to upload your app by clicking on **Submit**. If your game validated previously, then it should upload smoothly to iTunes Connect. Now your game should be one step closer to being available for either beta testing or purchase/download on the App Store.

Beta test your game with the TestFlight service

Every app should have at least some form of beta testing before release with video games usually being the type of apps that need it more than others, as games tend to have more variables and chances for crashing than your run-of-the-mill mobile program. Also, the Apple services, such as GameCenter and In-App purchases, can't be tested correctly without moving to this phase.

In the past, the only way to test iOS apps before release was using the ad hoc distribution method, validating individual devices with their UDID, and giving the testers a download with a manifest file that would allow the app to actually work on their device. This is where Apple differs greatly from other platforms such as Android. Apple is very careful in keeping what developers like to call a *walled garden* with their application distribution.

In the past, this was a bit of a headache and led to a rather convoluted ad hoc setup as compared with Android resulting in app bugs not being noted until after the release. To help keep the integrity of Apple's app distribution and give developers a better way of pretesting their apps easily and to have more people than the original 100 device limit, the TestFlight service was created. The TestFlight icon is seen here:

TestFlight Beta Testing

TestFight is an app that anybody can download from the Apple App store for their iOS device. For you, the developer, it can be a great tool for early distribution of your games. TestFlight testers are segmented into two groups: internal testers and external testers. Internal testers are made up of your own team members, and you can have a maximum of 25 internal testers.

In iTunes Connect, you can set roles for your team in the **Users and Roles** main section. These roles include Admin, Technical, Marketing, and others. The members that are in the Admin and Technical category are those whom you can assign as internal testers. Making those users internal testers is as easy as turning on the **Internal Testers** switch next to their name.

To have these users test your game in TestFlight, locate your game in the **My Apps** section of iTunes Connect. If your game's build was successfully added to iTunes Connect from the steps provided in the previous section, then you should see it listed in the **Prerelease** tab.

 When you upload your app to iTunes Connect they can be divided into versions, which are then subdivided into their own builds. For example, version 1.0 (1) is version 1.0, build 1 of your game, whereas 1.0(1.2) would be version 1.0 / build 1.2 of your game. Changing the build string in your project and then uploading that new build is how you can divide your app for this page in iTunes Connect. We will discuss more on this while creating a new update to your game, but this is the process for versioning the prerelease builds.

The next step is to click on the build or version, which should open the build's own metadata page. Fill in this information to better help your testers know whom to contact and what to test. This information is what your testers will see when they download your game's beta version.

To allow this build/version for TestFlight testing, simply switch on the **TestFlight Beta Testing** switch found on the upper-right side of the version's listing in the **Prerelease** tab.

Now to have your testers test this build in their TestFlight app, simply click on the **Internal Testers** tab next to the **Builds** tab on in the game's prerelease page, click on the checkmark next to their name and then click on **Invite**.

They should get an e-mail to accept that invite, and you will see which build they are testing once they installed it in TestFlight.

External tester invites

To get external testers for your game with TestFlight is also a rather simple process with one caveat; your app needs to be submitted for beta review. Doing so is simple though all you need to do is to click on the **Submit For Beta App Review** link at the right side of your app's build; again in the **Builds** tab of the **Prerelease** section.

As with the actual App Store submission, it might involve waiting before moving to the next step. The wait is not as long as the full app submission and is a very good sign that all will go well when you do the public release. Unlike internal testers, all of the metadata must be completed but you can have up to 1000 testers! You can start to invite testers once the **Submit For Beta App Review** link is tapped and your app is waiting for beta test review.

Now go to the **External Testers** tab in the **Prerelease** page and then click on the **+** button to add them with their e-mail address and (optionally) their first and last name. Click on **Next** to add that person to your invite list. Note that you only have 30 days for external testers to review that build of your game.

Once your app passes beta review, your external testers can test your app just like your internal testers can.

Analyzing crash reports and feedback from testers

Now that you have people testing your game, take notes from their e-mails on what issues there might be in your game and then go back to your game's project to do the needed fixes. Update the build number in the build string of your Xcode project and reupload the build to easily allow your testers to keep up to date with each new prerelease update.

App crash reports can be viewed in the **App Analytics** main section of iTunes Connect, as seen in the image from PikiPop's information as follows. However, it seems that these detailed crash analytics are for after release and not during prerelease.

More on TestFlight and even a video explanation can be found on Apple's official page on the subject as follows:

```
https://developer.apple.com/testflight/
```

Submitting your game for review

This is the point in your game's development you've worked so hard for, submitting it to the Apple App Store. The good news is that most of the work has already been done! To submit your game for review, at this point, all you have to do is go to your app's **Versions** tab and click on the **Submit For Review** tab.

You can see this in the following *Adventure app* example image:

You will be asked a few questions before the actual submission, such as about Export Compliance, Content rights, and **Advertising Identifier (IDFA)** information. More information on IDFA can be found here:

```
https://developer.apple.com/library/ios/documentation/
LanguagesUtilities/Conceptual/iTunesConnect_Guide/Chapters/
SubmittingTheApp.html#//apple_ref/doc/uid/TP40011225-CH33-SW8
```

Now the waiting game begins with your game in the *Waiting For Review* status. Again, the wait time for app approval will vary but is usually much less than it used to be in the past. Hopefully, all goes well and you will see a green mark stating your game's submitted version number with the words **Ready for Sale**; as follows:

Congrats! Your game should be now located in the App Store for everyone with an iOS device to download and play! Make sure to check out the various analytics tools iTunes Connect provides to keep a pulse on your game.

Updating your game

Games today are almost never a one-shot deal. They tend to be a living application through updates, add-ons, and fixes even after release. Updates to your app will be working to any future iOS updates, adding new game content, or a combination of both. To do this, simply repeat much of the processes from the *build string* phase starting with the creation of a new version number. Doing so will create a new section in your **Builds** tab under **Prerelease** as seen with PikiPop's own page as follows:

You can use TestFlight beta test to test the new build with internal and external testers just as you did before. To make ready the newest version for release, click on the **New Version** button on the **Versions** main tab and submit the newest version's number in the popup.

The **Versions** tab will now be divided into the current version and the new version via easy-to-navigate tabs. Like in the original release, you can fill in various metadata as well as information for the players for what this new update will entail. Submit the version for review and once approved, the newest game update will be in the app store that players will either automatically download or be notified about, based on their device's App Store update settings.

That about does it! If more game frameworks and tools come out in future versions of iOS, you can have them as part of your game with your updates. Making a great game even better is always the right choice for every game developer.

Summary

Throughout this chapter, we saw what was needed to finally take your game from an Xcode project to a playable game for everyone with an iOS device. We learned about the steps needed to set up our Xcode project before submission to iTunes Connect. Then, we got an introduction to TestFlight, which is a great service for us to beta test our games before release. We saw that those steps already prepared us for most of what was needed to submit our games for review. Finally, we saw how easy it was to create app updates in iTunes Connect.

You now have a game app that hopefully thousands of players can enjoy. No matter if the game was big or small, be proud of the fact that you created something for players to enjoy. Even the simplest of games can be a worthy accomplishment. We've seen throughout this book that the process of making an iOS game, though easier than even a few years ago, takes some effort and diligence to get right. This concludes all of the technical aspects we shall discuss. Next, we conclude with a quick discussion on the future of iOS and game development as a whole.

8
The Future of iOS Game Development

For the entirety of this book we have gone over the features from iOS 8 and the recent announcements of iOS 9. So, what of the future of iOS game development? Obviously, nobody can tell what the future will bring, but we can guess a few possibilities based on the recent evolution of the iOS/Xcode platform, programming, and how game development as a whole will change.

A greater focus on functional programming

As of this publication, the Swift programming language is only a year old but it represents a recent paradigm shift in much of programming. Object-oriented programming and design still holds true, but a shift to functional programming is where languages such as Scala and Swift place their focus. Functional programming, in summary, is a focus on functions being pure mathematical calculations of objects with an avoidance of the state changes and mutable data that we've seen with past languages, such as C++/Java and even Apple's own Objective-C. Instead of dealing with subroutines, a function only works on the parameters it's given. Swift does this well with its closures, which we've seen a few times in this book, and are often used to compact much of the logic in game programming for iOS.

Since *WWDC14*, Apple has told developers that Swift is the successor to both C and Objective-C. It's a completely rebuilt language from the ground up with speed and efficiency as its focus, something game developers must always take advantage of and why Swift is now the language of choice going forward for iOS game development. Objective-C is not going away, and Swift still has some growing up to do before it can even take over all of what Objective-C can do for iOS development. Swift's 2.0 update from iOS 9 added more for error catching and debugging with keywords, such as throw, catch, and guard. Thankfully, we don't have to abandon any past Objective-C projects since the ability to use both Swift and Objective-C in the same project is very simple through the use of an Objective-C/Swift Bridging file.

As we move on to future versions of iOS, expect more debugging controls and improvements to Swift's ability to compact detailed logic into a few lines. Some data sorting functionalities of Swift are faster than Objective-C, and in the world of game development, any gains in frame rate is always a good thing. Despite the advances in CPU/GPU power and the ever-growing ease of game development frameworks, such as SpriteKit and SceneKit, the design aspect of game design can be a double-edged sword if we forget the engineering aspect of this craft. Some of the tools given to us in the recent game development scene can make almost anybody a game developer. This is a good thing. We want people from all walks of life to be game developers, but we must not let some of the recent and future tools that allow games on iOS or other platforms making us lazy and forget that there is and always will be a programming/engineering side to this industry. The frameworks and visual tools of iOS and other game engines should always be treated as tools and never as a crutch. The best games of the past, present, and in the future will be games that tap into every aspect of game development, particularly, the hardest aspects of game development, such as the graphics pipeline. That's why Apple tapped into the details of the GPU with the Metal API.

The Apple Watch

As of iOS 9, the Apple Watch's platform already got an upgrade with watchOS 2. The Apple Watch is generally, at the moment, not a video game platform. Without taking the small screen size into play, apps made for the Apple Watch don't have much in the way of making game-like graphics updates. In the future, this might change. At the moment, apps made in watchOS are like child apps of main iOS apps. Eventually, we can make watchOS apps separately without having them attached to a parent iOS project. However, some developers have made simple text-based games for the Apple watch. It's possible that in the future, we could make more action-oriented games for the Apple Watch.

Currently, it's very much possible to make a game that uses the watch for accessories data, such as inventory, maps, and more with a little bit of ingenuity. One feature of the Apple Watch that we could design games or game controls with is **Force Touch**. Force Touch senses how firm the press gesture is. This isn't something new to game design as a whole but new to iOS with the next line of iPhones and iPads most likely having this feature as well. Getting the strength of a player's touch and taps could allow some intuitive gameplay mechanics for the next line of mobile games.

For more on the watchOS to possibly inspire some game development ideas for the device, check out the watchOS 2 preview page at `https://www.apple.com/watchos-2-preview/`.

Component-based structuring

We saw in the previous chapters that iOS has imparted much of the component-based structuring paradigm to tackle the unique software/programming requirements that come from game development. Instead of building a tall parent-child structure that we see from an object-oriented design, it builds a structure that does best by growing it's structure in width. Classes, such as `GKEntity`, `GKComponent`, and other aspects of `GameplayKit`, are what let us take advantage of these features. This type of structuring isn't all too new in game development. Component-based structuring has been used by multiplatform game engines, such as Unity and Unreal Engine, and continues to be the way game developers like us make and reuse parts of our games. Expect the future updates to Xcode and iOS to utilize these features even more. In the near future, we will probably see Xcode look and act even more like these game engines but with the benefit of being specifically made for the iOS devices, allowing even deeper, custom integration. Doing all of this directly in Xcode and with iOS frameworks allows instant access to Apple features without the use of paid asset tools or waiting for plugin updates. Developers for the next generation of iOS games will be able to take AI actions, character abilities, HUD animations, and other features made in one game and reuse them almost instantly for a completely different game. Component-based structuring makes it where the developer can build a library of reusable features by placing the design of our games ahead of typical development hurdles.

The rise of VR

This has been a topic that Apple has been rather quiet about where other platforms have been rather vocal. Even the manufacturers of Apple's A7/A8 chips, Samsung, have joined the VR development environment with their GearVR device and their partnership with Oculus on the project. Google has created the simple Cardboard setup, akin to the GearVR, which simply lets the user place their smartphone into the device or box to experience VR experiences and games. Most famously, there is the Oculus Rift, which will have its consumer model available in the first quarter of 2016, and will likely be the front runner in this newer game environment.

Virtual reality is a topic that has come up a number of times in the past few decades. It has come and gone, but for the time being, it seems to be getting its overdue foothold in technology. The Unity game engine, for example, just recently allowed for native support of VR. The thought process in making these games is a bit different and has yet to be fully fleshed out. It is possible that soon Apple will throw their hat into this arena. If you haven't already, learning how to make fun games in the VR space might be a worthy act of foresight.

Summary

We hope that the discussions and tutorials seen throughout this book helped you either learn the platform for the first time or enriched what you might have already known about iOS. We hope that you take this knowledge and make some amazing games for the iOS family of devices and continue to learn more about the platform and game development as a whole.

In the end, always remember that game design and programming is a combination of computer science, engineering, art, and lots of hard work. It's a complex creative field that is a combination of every other creative profession from music to movie making, to 2D animation, 3D sculpting, and more. As the case with other creative fields, developers should never feel *done* and always be humble in what they know and acknowledge that there's always more to learn in this ever-growing field. Like a videogame, be up for the challenge. Realize when you look back that you essentially leveled up from what you used to know and there are always more abilities to gain.

Index

Thank you for buying
iOS 9 Game Development Essentials

About Packt Publishing

Packt, pronounced 'packed', published its first book, *Mastering phpMyAdmin for Effective MySQL Management*, in April 2004, and subsequently continued to specialize in publishing highly focused books on specific technologies and solutions.

Our books and publications share the experiences of your fellow IT professionals in adapting and customizing today's systems, applications, and frameworks. Our solution-based books give you the knowledge and power to customize the software and technologies you're using to get the job done. Packt books are more specific and less general than the IT books you have seen in the past. Our unique business model allows us to bring you more focused information, giving you more of what you need to know, and less of what you don't.

Packt is a modern yet unique publishing company that focuses on producing quality, cutting-edge books for communities of developers, administrators, and newbies alike. For more information, please visit our website at www.packtpub.com.

About Packt Open Source

In 2010, Packt launched two new brands, Packt Open Source and Packt Enterprise, in order to continue its focus on specialization. This book is part of the Packt Open Source brand, home to books published on software built around open source licenses, and offering information to anybody from advanced developers to budding web designers. The Open Source brand also runs Packt's Open Source Royalty Scheme, by which Packt gives a royalty to each open source project about whose software a book is sold.

Writing for Packt

We welcome all inquiries from people who are interested in authoring. Book proposals should be sent to author@packtpub.com. If your book idea is still at an early stage and you would like to discuss it first before writing a formal book proposal, then please contact us; one of our commissioning editors will get in touch with you.

We're not just looking for published authors; if you have strong technical skills but no writing experience, our experienced editors can help you develop a writing career, or simply get some additional reward for your expertise.

open source
community experience distilled

PUBLISHING

Learning iOS 8 Game Development Using Swift

ISBN: 978-1-78439-355-7   Paperback: 366 pages

Create robust and spectacular 2D and 3D games from scratch using Swift – Apple's latest and easy-to-learn programming language

1. Create engaging games from the ground up using SpriteKit and SceneKit.

2. Boost your game's visual performance using Metal - Apple's new graphics library.

3. A step-by-step approach to exploring the world of game development using Swift.

Mastering Cocos2d Game Development

ISBN: 978-1-78439-671-8   Paperback: 290 pages

Master game development with Cocos2d to develop amazing mobile games for iOS

1. Learn how to create beautiful and engaging mobile games using Cocos2D-Swift.

2. Explore the cross-platform capabilities of Cocos2d.

3. Get to grips with Cocos2d game development tools and learn Swift, a powerful modern approach to game development.

Please check **www.PacktPub.com** for information on our titles

iOS Game Programming Cookbook

ISBN: 978-1-78439-825-5   Paperback: 300 pages

Over 45 interesting game recipes that will help you create your next enthralling game

1. Learn to create 2D graphics with Sprite Kit, game physics, AI behaviours, 3D game programming, and multiplayer gaming.

2. Use native iOS frameworks for OpenGL to create 3D textures, allowing you to explore 3D animations and game programming.

3. Explore powerful iOS game features through detailed step-by-step recipes.

Learning Unreal® Engine iOS Game Development

ISBN: 978-1-78439-771-5   Paperback: 212 pages

Create exciting iOS games with the power of the new Unreal® Engine 4 subsystems

1. Learn each step in the iOS game development process, from start to finish.

2. Develop exciting iOS games with the Unreal Engine 4.x toolset.

3. Step-by-step tutorials to build optimized iOS games.

Please check **www.PacktPub.com** for information on our titles

www.ingramcontent.com/pod-product-compliance
Lightning Source LLC
Chambersburg PA
CBHW060553060326
40690CB00017B/3697